RUSSIAN
GRAMMAR MADE EASY

A Comprehensive Workbook
To Learn Russian Grammar
For Beginners (Audio Included)

Lingo Mastery

CONTENTS

INTRODUCTION

Dear reader, if this book has attracted your attention, then you have decided to face the challenge of learning Russian – one of the most complicated languages in the world. Spoken by over 155 million people all over the globe, this language is a gateway to a new culture, new friends, and new horizons of travelling, business, and self-development. This book may well become one of the keys to unlock these gates.

By calling Russian a complicated language, we don't mean to intimidate you and would rather prefer to focus on the word "easy" in the title. Of course, "easy" doesn't guarantee an effort-free and error-proof experience. For us, this word means that the way toward the goal is logical, adequate to beginner – lower intermediate level, and oriented toward implementing the knowledge in real-life situations.

Furthermore, Russian people are often claimed to be unfriendly and even rude. The assumption is driven from the fact that they rarely smile and are not very eager to communicate with strangers. However, many people, including scientists, contradict this fact. The thing is that Russians are really sincere people, and mostly express their emotions when they are strong, deep, and usually directed to someone they know. Once you know Russian people better, you'll be surprised by their hospitality and interest toward the interlocutor.

The same refers to the Russian language – it can seem hostile and unapproachable, but some time, effort, and diligence will reveal a beautiful world of new ways to express things and look at the world. We're here to help you discover this beauty in a fun, comprehensive, and efficient way.

WHAT DOES THIS BOOK OFFER?

This book features basic grammar rules that are essential for speaking and comprehension. Fairly called one of the most difficult grammar systems, Russian grammar is all about word endings and exceptions, but we tried hard to offer you its most crucial part that will be enough for a start and not too much to overwhelm you.

We also believe that no learned rule makes sense until its use is chiseled in practice, so you'll have plenty of exercises to make your theoretical knowledge applicable in life.

The book comprises four chapters, each of which is divided into parts with theoretical and practical sections.

The theoretical parts include:

- Grammar rules
- Examples
- Round-up tables
- Essential notes and hacks

The practical parts include various exercises, including:

- Matching
- Multiple choice
- Creating grammar forms
- Images
- Audio
- Miscellaneous practice after each chapter

HOW TO MAKE THE MOST OUT OF THIS BOOK

- **Take your time**

  We want you to remember that we offer grammar not for the sake of knowing many rules, but for the sake of being able to speak and understand others – efficient communication is our major goal. So, no one expects you to remember all the words, constructions, endings, and peculiarities right away. Feel free to go back to the theory section as many times as needed, to look up words in the dictionary and to see how to build grammatical structures you need.

- **When doing an exercise, you're not sitting an exam**

  The goal of the exercises is to help you understand how things work, so use all the information you have and don't be afraid to make a mistake.

- **Wait before checking the translation**

  Many exercises are accompanied by English translations to minimize dictionary consultations and to give you a chance to compare, spot differences, and see how the language works instead of experiencing the frustration of constantly referring to a dictionary. However, we recommend challenging yourself as much as you can before turning to the translation. Moreover, after you do, don't be in a hurry to progress to the next task. Compare, analyze, and develop all language skills while you focus on grammar.

· **Make sure you get all the value from the conversations**

While many conversations in the book miss words or require forms to be created, filling in and arranging is not the only thing to do with them. Conversations are full of useful expressions that you can use in real life. So, make sure you act them out and devote enough effort to compare them with the English translations.

WHAT GRAMMAR WILL I LEARN IN THIS BOOK?

This book includes the following units:

· Nouns
· Pronouns
· Adjectives
· Verbs

Now that you know what to expect from this book, you can take the first step that will be followed by thousands of others. The journey may be hard, but remember to keep going; focus on your achievements, no matter how small they seem; and learn from your failures instead of letting them hold you back. You've already started and that's a huge part of every successful mission!

HOW TO GET THE AUDIO FILES

Some of the exercises throughout this book come with accompanying audio files. You can download these audio files if you head over to
www.lingomastery.com/russian-gme-audio

1

NOUNS

CHAPTER

Genuinely the heart of any language, nouns are logical to start with when learning grammar. In Russian, nouns change according to gender, number, and cases, and require other parts of speech like pronouns and adjectives to agree with them in these categories. We'll start with the easiest part, which is the gender and go on to learn the cases – something most foreign learners find intimidating, but which just takes diligence and practice to master.

PART I
THE GENDER AND NUMBER OF NOUNS

GENDER

There are three genders in Russian:

- masculine;
- feminine;
- neuter (neutral).

Very often grammatical gender is attributed to the noun according to physical gender, like in "девочка" - "girl," which is feminine.

With other nouns, especially inanimate ones, it's different and the good news is that you don't need to memorize the gender of each noun (like in German, for example). The gender can easily be defined by an ending of the noun in its initial form, apart from a few exceptions that we'll cover later.

To define the gender of a noun, take a look at the ending.

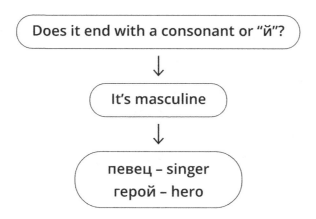

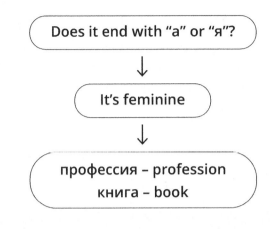

Does it end with "а" or "я"?

↓

It's feminine

↓

профессия – profession
книга – book

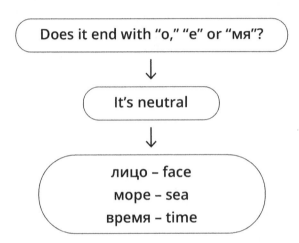

Does it end with "о," "е" or "мя"?

↓

It's neutral

↓

лицо – face
море – sea
время – time

 Groups of exceptions to remember:

1. **Nouns ending with "ь" (soft sign)**

    They can be either masculine or feminine. Generally speaking, the gender of such nouns should be memorized, but still it's possible to form certain groups.

    · **The following nouns that end with "ь" are always masculine:**

    ✓ Names of months (октябр**ь** – October, июн**ь** – June)
    ✓ Nouns that end with "арь" (календ**арь** – calendar)
    ✓ Nouns that end with "тель" (учи**тель** – teacher)

    · **Nouns that end with "чь," "шь," "щь" are feminine**
    ноч**ь** – night
    чуш**ь** – nonsense

2. Nouns that end with "а" or "я," but are masculine due to physical gender:

папа – dad
дядя – uncle
дедушка – grandfather
мужчина – man

NUMBER

Just like in English, Russian nouns can be both singular and plural. The plural form depends on the ending of the noun in its initial form (nominative case singular) and the gender of this noun. So, you first need to identify the gender, then spot the ending, and finally make the corresponding changes. There are also a number of exceptions to memorize.

SINGULAR AND PLURAL FORMS OF NOUNS

GENDER	ENDING CHANGES	EXAMPLES
Masculine	Consonant – cons. + "ы"*	велосипед – велосипеды bike – bikes
Masculine	"й" turns into "и"	музей – музеи museum – museums
Masculine	"ь" turns into "и"	шампунь – шампуни shampoo – shampoos
Feminine	"а" turns into "ы"**	мама – мамы mom – moms
Feminine	"я" turns into "и"	неделя – недели week – weeks
Feminine	"ия" turns into "ии"	коллекция – коллекции collection – collections
Feminine	"ь" turns into "и"	ночь – ночи night – nights
Neutral	"о" turns into "а"	окно – окна window – windows
Neutral	"е" turns into "я"	море – моря sea – seas
Neutral	"ие" turns into "ия"	желание – желания wish – wishes
Neutral	"мя" turns into "ена"	имя – имена name – names

*There are exceptions to this rule. The following words take **"a"/"я" instead of "ы"**:

доктор (doctor) – доктор**а**   город (city) – город**а**

адрес (address) – адрес**а**   паспорт (passport) – паспорт**а**

вечер (evening) – вечер**а**   поезд (train) – поезд**а**

глаз (eye) – глаз**а**   учитель (teacher) – учител**я**

If the ending is preceded by **г, к, х, ж, ч, ш, or щ, the plural form is created with the ending **"и"** instead of **"ы."**

Example: мальчик – мальчик**и** (boy – boys)
          книга – книг**и** (book – books)

NOUNS THAT ARE ALWAYS PLURAL

деньги – money

брюки – trousers (formal piece of clothes, part of a suit)

штаны – pants (casual piece of clothes)

ботинки – shoes

часы – watches, clock

ножницы – scissors

духи – perfume

каникулы – holidays

шахматы – chess

очки – glasses

ворота – gates

NOUNS THAT ARE ALWAYS SINGULAR

1. Uncountable substances; for example, вода (water), свет (light), молоко (milk).

2. Abstract notions, feelings, and emotions; for example, любовь (love), радость (joy), грусть (sadness).

3. Collective nouns, like мебель (furniture), посуда (tablewear), обувь (shoes).

Note that sometimes the native language can trick you. For example, "hair" in English is always singular (unless we mean separate hairs), while in Russian "волосы" is always plural (unless we mean a separate hair). "Police" is always plural in English, while in Russian "полиция" is always singular.

NOUNS THAT COINCIDE IN SINGULAR AND PLURAL

метро (underground) – метро
пианино (piano) – пианино
кофе (coffee) – кофе
хобби (hobby) – хобби
пальто (coat) – пальто
радио (radio) – радио
шоссе (highway) – шоссе
меню (menu) – меню

IRREGULAR PLURALS

мать (mother) – мат**ери**
дочь (daughter) – доч**ери**
ребёнок (child) – **дети**
цветок (flower) – цвет**ы**
яблоко (apple) – яблок**и**
человек (person) – **люди**

NOUNS THAT TAKE THE ENDING "ья" IN PLURAL

дерево (tree) – дерев**ья**
брат (brother) – брат**ья**
друг (friend) – друз**ья**
сын (son) – сынов**ья**
крыло (wing) – крыл**ья**
лист (leaf) – лист**ья**
стул (chair) – стул**ья**

EXERCISES

1. Use a dictionary to fill in the English equivalents of the words in the images and define their gender.

платье

1. _____

окно

5. _____

дом

2. _____

девушка

6. _____

строитель

3. _____

календарь

7. _____

пламя

4. _____

дедушка

8. _____

2. Identify the gender of nouns and tick the right table.

NOUN	MASCULINE	FEMININE	NEUTRAL
ночь – night			
время – time			
герой – hero			
лицо – face			
зима – winter			
музей – museum			
станция – station			
шоколад – chocolate			
фотография – photo			
январь – January			
кошка – cat			
море – sea			
стол – table			
кафе – café			
машина – car			
дядя – uncle			
апрель – April			
семья – family			
друг – friend			

3. Create plural forms of the nouns in the images.

собака

1. _____

яйцо

2. _____

музей

3. _____

глаз

4. _____

ребёнок

5. _____

пальто

6. _____

фотография

7. _____

дерево

8. _____

4. Create the correct plural form of the noun in brackets.

1. Эти (здание) похожи друг на друга. _____
   These buildings are similar to each other.

2. Ты не забыл забрать (газета) из почтового ящика? _____
   Did you remember to take the newspapers out of the mailbox?

3. Возьми свои (слово) обратно! _____
   Take your words back!

4. Эти мальчики – мои (брат). _____
   These boys are my brothers.

5. Я терпеть не могу (каша). _____
   I hate porridges!

6. Какие красивые (цветок)! _____
   What beautiful flowers!

7. Эти (письмо) от моего брата. _____
   These letters are from my brother.

8. В детстве ему нравились (история) дедушки. _____
   Back in his childhood, he liked his grandfather's stories.

9. (Человек) бывают очень жестоки. _____
   People can be very cruel.

10. Купи (лимон) по дороге домой, пожалуйста. _____
    Buy some lemons on your way home please.

11. Меня всегда интересовали (поезд). _____
    I have always been interested in trains.

12. Летние (вечер) тёплые и тихие. _____
    Summer evenings are warm and quiet.

5. Group the nouns into two columns and use these words to complete the sentences below.

| деньги | вода | очки | брюки | мебель |
| посуда | часы | молоко | ножницы | любовь |

ALWAYS SINGULAR	ALWAYS PLURAL

1. Тебе нравится _____ в этой комнате?

2. Дай мне _____, пожалуйста. Я хочу разрезать бумагу.

3. _____ — это очень сильное чувство.

4. Мне нужны мои _____. Я ничего не вижу.

5. Это _____ моего дедушки, но они не работают.

6. Не пей! Эта _____ грязная.

7. В этом рецепте есть _____?

8. Мои _____ в шкафу?

9. У тебя есть _____ на отпуск?

10. Вся _____ чистая! Это ты помыл её?

6. Complete the conversations with the words from the boxes. Pay attention to the fact that you will need to make plural forms yourself. Then check yourself with the audio. (Find audio on page 3.)

CONVERSATION I

адрес   кресло   семья   трамвай   общежитие
ключ   комната   студент   кровать

А: Привет! Как дела с квартирой?

В: Привет! Не очень. Не могу найти хороший вариант.

А: Возле моего дома есть два **1)** _____. Говорят, там хорошие **2)** _____.

В: Здорово! Можешь дать мне их **3)** _____?

А: Конечно! Тебе там понравится. Там живут **4)** _____ и **5)** _____.

Через два дня...

А: Ты нашёл комнату?

В: О, да! Спасибо! Вот **6)** _____! Там даже есть мебель.

А: Правда?

В: Да, две **7)** _____ и два **8)** _____.

А: Немного странно.

В: Да, но я рад. Тем более, здание близко к университету и рядом ходят **9)** _____.

А: Я рад, что смог помочь тебе!

А: Hi! How are things going with the apartment?

В: Hi! Not quite well. I can't find a good option.

А: There are two dormitories next to my house. They say they have good rooms there.

В: Great! Can you give me their addresses?

А: Sure! You'll like it there. Families and students live there.

Two days later...

A: Have you found a room?

B: Oh, yes! Thank you! Here are the keys! They even have furniture there.

A: Really?

B: Yes, two beds and two chairs.

A: A bit strange.

B: Yeah, but I'm happy. Moreover, the building is close to the university and there is a tram route there.

A: I'm glad I was able to help you!

 **CONVERSATION II**

> виза   мальчик   сын   нож   доктор

A: Привет, Лена! Давно не виделись!

B: Привет, Таня! Рада тебя видеть!

A: Как твои **1)** _____?

B: Спасибо, хорошо. Мои **2)** _____ **3)** _____.

A: Здорово! В какой больнице они работают?

B: Они не работают у нас. Они сделали рабочие **4)** _____ и уехали в Польшу.

A: Молодцы!

B: А как твой сын?

A: Мой сын шеф-повар. Видишь эти **5)** _____ у меня в сумке? Это его подарок на день рождения.

B: Ух ты! Ему понравится!

A: Надеюсь!

A: Hi Lena! Long time no see!

B: Hi Tanya! Glad to see you!

A: How are your boys doing?

B: Fine, thanks. My sons are doctors.

A: Great! What hospital do they work in?

B: They don't work in our town. They received working visas and left for Poland.

A: Good for them!

B: And how is your son doing?

A: My son is a chef. See these knives in my bag? It's a birthday present for him.

B: Wow! He's going to like them!

A: Hope so!

PART II
THE CASES OF NOUNS

There are six cases in the Russian language and all of them make nouns change their endings accordingly. When mastering cases, it's important to focus on two major directions:

1. How a certain case is formed

2. When a certain case should be used

We will now cover all cases, first explaining what they mean and how to understand in which situations they should be used and then providing two tables with ending changes – one for singular nouns and the other for plural nouns. The exception will be the nominative case only as it's the initial form of the noun.

ИМЕНИТЕЛЬНЫЙ ПАДЕЖ – NOMINATIVE CASE

Indicates: The subject of the sentence.

Notes: All the nouns in Russian dictionaries are in the nominative case. So, the only changes that can occur are when a noun takes a plural form.

Example:

Мой брат часто опаздывает на работу. – **My brother** is often late for work.
Мой дом далеко от офиса. – **My house** is far away from the office.

РОДИТЕЛЬНЫЙ ПАДЕЖ – GENITIVE CASE

Nouns are used in the genitive case in the following situations:

1. **To indicate possession with the possessor always following the object he/she/ it possesses.**

   Это машина **папы**. – This is **dad's** car.
   Это дом наших **родителей**. – This is our **parents'** house.

2. **After numerals with certain numerals followed by genitive singular and others by genitive plural.**

- We use genitive singular after numerals 2, 3, and 4 and all other numerals ending with these numbers, except for 12, 13, and 14.

  У неё **четыре сына**. – She has **four sons**.
  В этой компании **пятьдесят три работника**. – This company has **fifty-three employees**.

- We use genitive plural after numerals from 5 to 9 and all the numerals ending with these numbers and after numeral 10.

  Мне нужно закончить **пять докладов**. – I need to finish **five reports**.
  Я купила **восемнадцать книг**. – I've bought **eighteen books**.

3. **After nouns denoting quantity, including:**

- мало – few/little
- много – much/many/a lot of
- несколько – a few/some
- сколько – how many/how much

  У нас **мало сахара**. – We've got **little sugar**.
  У меня есть **несколько** редких **картин**. – I have a few **rare paintings**.

4. **After measure words, such as:**

- чашка – a cup (of)
- бутылка – a bottle (of)
- литр – liter (of)
- кусок – a piece (of)
- килограмм – a kilo (of)

  Дайте мне **бутылку воды**, пожалуйста. – Give me **a bottle of water**, please.
  Хочешь **кусок пирога**? – Would you like **a piece of pie**?

5. **To indicate part of a substance or liquid or an indefinite quantity.**

  In English you would use "some" for the purpose, while in Russian there is no need to add any word – a genitive case form is enough.

  Он выпил **лимонада**. – He drank **some lemonade**.
  Хочешь **чая**? – Would you like some **tea**?

6. After the negation "нет" to indicate that something either doesn't exist or is absent.

У нас **нет помидоров** для салата. – We **don't have any tomatoes** for the salad.
На Марсе **нет воды**. – There is **no water** on Mars.

7. With the preposition "у" and the "verb "есть" to indicate that someone has something.

У моей **сестры** есть хомяк. – My **sister** has a hamster.
У наших **соседей** есть внуки. – Our **neighbors** have grandchildren.

8. After the following prepositions:

✓ без – without
✓ для – for
✓ кроме – besides, except
✓ вместо – instead of
✓ из – from, out of
✓ с – from, off
✓ от – from

✓ у – at
✓ вокруг – around
✓ напротив – opposite
✓ около – near
✓ внутри – inside
✓ до – before
✓ после – after

Их дом **около реки**. – Their house is **near the river**.
Она достала котёнка **из сумки**. – She took a kitten **out of the bag**.

THE SINGULAR FORM OF THE GENITIVE CASE

GENDER	ENDING CHANGES	EXAMPLES
Masculine	Consonant – cons. + "а"	Велосипе**д** – Bike У меня нет велосипед**а**. I don't have a bike.
	"й" turns into "я"	Хокк**ей** – Hockey Я не фанат хокке**я**. I am not a hockey fan.
	"ь" turns into "я"	Коктейл**ь** – Cocktail Хочешь клубничного коктей**ля**? Would you like some strawberry cocktail?

Feminine	"a" turns into "ы"*	Мам**а** – Mom Ты пришёл без мам**ы**? Did you come without your mom?
Neutral	"я" turns into "и"	Тёт**я** – Aunt Это дом моей тёт**и**. This is my aunt's house.
	"ия" turns into "ии"	Полиц**ия** – Police Здесь нет полиц**ии**. There are no police here.
	"ь" turns into "и"	Обув**ь** – Shoes У неё нет зимней обув**и**. She doesn't have winter shoes.
	"о" turns into "а"	Окн**о** – Window Я вижу тебя из окн**а**. I see you out of the window.
	"е" turns into "я"	Мор**е** – Sea Это фотография мор**я**. This is a photo of the sea.
	"мя" turns into "мени"	Им**я** – Name У моего щенка ещё нет и**мени**. My puppy doesn't have a name yet.
	"ие" turns into "ия"	Желан**ие** – Wish У меня нет желан**ия** идти на прогулку. I don't have any wish to go for a walk.

* According to the spelling rules, consonants **г, к, х, ж, ч, ш,** and **щ** are never followed by the vowel **"ы,"** so feminine nouns that have these consonants before the ending take **"и"** instead of **"ы."**

Example: книг**а** - книг**и**
У меня нет этой книг**и**. – I don't have this book.

IRREGULAR GENITIVE

мат**ь** – мат**ери** (mother)   доч**ь** – доч**ери** (daughter)

Note that the nouns that end in **"а"** and **"я,"** but are masculine according to their physical gender (like папа, дедушка, дядя), form their endings like feminine nouns.

Я не хожу в школу без пап**ы**. – I don't go to school without my dad.

THE PLURAL FORM OF THE GENITIVE CASE

GENDER	ENDING CHANGES	EXAMPLES
Masculine	Consonant – cons. + "ов"*	Вопро**с** – Question У меня много вопрос**ов**. I've got a lot of questions.
	"й" turns into "ев"	Геро**й** – Hero Сейчас нет геро**ев**. There are no heroes nowadays.
	"ь" turns into "ей"	Учител**ь** – Teacher У нас в школе мало учител**ей**. We've got few teachers at our school.
Feminine	the ending "а" is removed**	Племянниц**а** – Niece Почему ты пришла без своих племянниц? Why did you come without your nieces?
	"я" turns into "ь"	Нян**я** – Babysitter В агентстве нет свободных нян**ь**. They don't have available babysitters at the agency.
	"ия" turns into "ий"	Виктор**ия** – Victoria (female name) У нас в офисе нет Виктор**ий**. Вы ошиблись. There are no Victorias at our office. You're mistaken.
	"ь" turns into "ей"	Бол**ь** – Pain (can be plural in Russian) У меня больше нет бол**ей** в спине. I don't have any pain in my back anymore.

Neutral	the ending "o" is removed	Лиц**о** – Face Здесь так много знакомых **лиц**! There are so many familiar faces here!
	"е" turns into "ей"	Мор**е** – Sea В нашей стране нет мор**ей**. There are no seas in our country.
	"я" turns into "ён"	Им**я** – Name Я не могу запомнить столько им**ён**. I can't remember so many names.
	"ие" turns into "ий"	Желан**ие** – Wish Ты загадал так много желан**ий**! You made so many wishes!

*If a masculine noun ends in **ж, ч, ш,** or **щ,** they take the ending **"ей"** instead of **"ов"**.

Example: Му**ж** – нет муж**ей** (Husband – no husbands)
Вра**ч** – нет врач**ей** (Doctor – no doctors)

** If the noun ends in a consonant cluster after the ending is removed, place **"е/о"** between these consonants.

For example: Девушк**а** – девуш**к** – много девуш**е**к (Girlfriend – many girlfriends)

IRREGULAR FORMS OF GENITIVE PLURAL

братья (brothers) – брать**ев**
друзья (friends) – друз**ей**
сыновья (sons) – сынов**ей**
англичане (Englishmen) – англичан
дочери (daughters) – дочер**ей**
матери (mothers) – матер**ей**
дети (children) – дет**ей**
люди (people) – люд**ей**

ДАТЕЛЬНЫЙ ПАДЕЖ – DATIVE CASE

Nouns are used in the dative case in the following situations:

1. To indicate an indirect object

An indirect object is a thing or a person to whom or for whom the action is done. In the example below "письмо" is a direct object, while "сестра" is an indirect one.

Я даю письмо **сестре**. – I'm giving the letter **to my sister**.

2. To express feelings and emotions

A noun denoting a person or any other living being that experiences a feeling or emotion should be in the dative case. In English, such phrases correspond to the "subject + to be + adjective" pattern, while in Russian it's "subject in dative + adverb."

Мальчику страшно. – **The boy** is scared.
Детям весело. – **The kids** are having fun.

3. To talk about age

The noun that denotes a person or an object whose age is described should be in the dative case.

Моей **бабушке** шестьдесят три года. – My **grandmother** is sixty-three years old.
Его **племяннику** десять. – His **nephew** is ten.

4. With the verbs "нравится - like" and "не нравится - dislike"

The noun that denotes a person who likes something should be in the dative case.

Детям нравится шоколад. – **Kids** like chocolate.
Моей **маме** не нравятся розы. – My **mom** dislikes roses.

Note that we say
"нрав**ит**ся/не нрав**ит**ся" in conjunction with singular nouns (all genders)
"нрав**ят**ся/не нрав**ят**ся" in conjunction with plural nouns (all genders)

5. **With the verb "нужно" to indicate that someone needs something**

The noun that denotes the person who needs something should be in the dative case, while the object they need should be in the nominative. The verb "нужно" can also be followed by a verb in the infinitive form.

Антону нужно купить билеты на поезд. – **Anton** needs to buy tickets for the train.
Маше нужны новые джинсы. – **Masha** needs new jeans.

Forms of the verb "нужно":

- нужно - in conjunction with a verb in the infinitive form or in conjunction with singular neutral nouns
- нужны - in conjunction with plural nouns (all genders)
- нужна - in conjunction with singular feminine nouns
- нужен - in conjunction with singular masculine nouns

6. **After the preposition "к," which means 'to'/'toward'**

Завтра я иду к **дантисту**. – I'm going **to** my **dentist** tomorrow.
На каникулы мы едем **к дедушке**. – We're going **to our grandfather's** for the holidays.

7. **After the preposition "по" that has several meanings:**

a. "about" or "on," usually to indicate to what area of knowledge a subject relates;

Это учебник **по химии**. – It's a textbook **on chemistry**.

b. "along" or "on" when there is movement involved;

Мы идём **по дороге**. – We're going **along the road**.
Насекомое ползёт **по листу**. – The insect is crawling **on a leaf**.

c. "over," "on," or "by" when it's about the means with which we do something.

Давай созвонимся **по скайпу**! – Let's have a call **over Skype**!
Я разговариваю **по телефону**. – I'm talking **on the phone**.

d. After the following verbs:

давать – give   помогать – help
звонить – call   желать – wish
советовать – advise

Note that these verbs don't form some rules but are listed here to help you memorize the most common cases.

Желаю вашей **команде** удачи! – I wish good luck to your **team**!
Вы можете посоветовать **туристам** интересное место? – Can you advise **the tourists** on an interesting place?

THE SINGULAR FORM OF THE DATIVE CASE

GENDER	ENDING CHANGES	EXAMPLES
Masculine	Consonant – cons. + "у"	Бра**т** – Brother Я купил бра**ту** новую книгу. I've bought a new book for my brother.
Masculine	"й" turns into "ю"	Гер**ой** – Hero Он помог геро**ю**. He has helped the hero.
Masculine	"ь" turns into "ю"	Строител**ь** – Builder Мы отдали материалы строител**ю**. We've given the materials to the builder.
Feminine	"а" turns into "е"	Сестр**а** – Sister Я подарю сестр**е** это платье. I will give this dress as a present to my sister.
Feminine	"я" turns into "е"	Тё**тя** – Aunt Удели внимание тёт**е**, пожалуйста. Pay some attention to your aunt, please.
Feminine	"ия" turns into "ии"	Мар**ия** – Mary Это письмо отправили Мар**ии**. This letter has been sent to Mary.
Feminine	"ь" turns into "и"	Ноч**ь** – Night Я рассказываю свои секреты только ноч**и**. I only share my secrets with the night.

Neutral	"o" turns into "y"	Лиц**о** – Face Приложи лёд к лиц**у**. Put some ice on your face.
	"e" turns into "ю"	Мор**е** – Sea Мор**ю** не нужен наш мусор. The sea doesn't need our garbage.
	"мя" turns into "мени"	И**мя** – Name Зови её по и**мени**, пожалуйста. Call her by her name, please.

IRREGULAR DATIVE

Мать – дать что-то мате**ри** (Mother – give something to mother)

Дочь – дать что-то доч**ери** (Daughter – give something to daughter)

THE PLURAL FORM OF THE DATIVE CASE

GENDER	ENDING CHANGES	EXAMPLE
Masculine **Feminine** **Neutral**	Consonant + "ам"	Вра**г** – Enemy Мы не отдадим золото враг**ам**! We won't give up the gold to our enemies!
	"a" turns into "ам"	Дедушк**а** – Grandfather. Мы купим нашим дедушк**ам** конфеты. We'll buy sweets for our grandfathers.
	"o" turns into "ам"	Письм**о** – Letter Удели немного времени письм**ам**! Devote some time to letters!
	"й" turns into "ям"	Геро**й** – Hero Дети подарили геро**ям** цветы. Kids gave flowers to heroes.
	"ь" turns into "ям"	Пекар**ь** – Baker Мы привезли муку пекар**ям**. We've brought flour to the bakers.
	"e" turns into "ям"	Мор**е** – Sea Он отдал свою жизнь мор**ям**. He gave his life to the seas.
	"я" turns into "ям"	Дяд**я** – Uncle Мы показали дяд**ям** новый фильм. We showed our uncles a new movie.

Note that dative plural forms don't depend on the gender of the noun. Instead, they depend on the ending of the noun in nominative singular.

IRREGULAR DATIVE PLURAL FORMS

братья (brothers) – братья**м**   дочери (daughters) – дочеря**м**   дети (children) – детя**м**

друзья (friends) – друзья**м**   матери (mothers) – матеря**м**   люди (people) – людя**м**

сыновья (sons) – сыновья**м**

ВИНИТЕЛЬНЫЙ ПАДЕЖ – ACCUSATIVE CASE

Nouns are used in the accusative case in the following situations:

1. To indicate a direct object

Unlike an indirect object that was mentioned above, a direct object is a thing or a person that is directly affected by the action, without any "middlemen." Here are some of the common verbs that are followed by direct objects:

знать – know   ненавидеть – hate

видеть – see   помнить – remember

слышать – hear   забыть – forget/leave somewhere

любить – love/like

Она забыла **кошелёк** в такси. – She left her **purse** in the taxi.

Я помню этого **парня**! – I remember this **guy**!

2. After the following prepositions:

в – to, into (direction)   под – under (direction)   про – about

на – on, onto (direction)   за – behind (direction)   через – through

Ученики идут **в школу**. – The pupils are going **to school**.

Это статья в газете **про мою дочь**. – This article in the newspaper is **about my daughter**.

3. Time expressions with "весь - all" and "каждый - every"

These words are followed by certain time periods expressed through nouns, like "минута," "час," "день," "неделя," "месяц," "год," "лето," "осень," "весна," "зима."

Всю **неделю** будет холодно. – It's going to be cold all week.

Она проверяет почту каждый **час**. – She checks her mail every hour.

The tricky part here is that the words "весь" and "каждый" change their forms according to the gender of the noun that denotes the time period. Here is a little crib note for you:

час, день, месяц, год – masculine – весь/каждый

минута, неделя, осень, весна, зима – feminine – вся/каждая

лето – neutral – всё/каждое

4. **To express physical state**

Unlike with the dative case, the accusative case is used when a feeling is expressed through an impersonal verb rather than an adverb.

Девушку знобит. – **The girl** has chills.
Мальчика тошнит. – **The boy** feels nauseated.

When it comes to ending changes, many forms of the accusative case coincide with the previously studied forms and take minimum memorizing of new endings. For easy and correct formation of the accusative case forms, it is necessary to divide the nouns into two groups: animate and inanimate objects.

ACCUSATIVE CASE FOR ANIMATE OBJECTS

Animate objects are living beings, including people and animals.

ANIMATE NOUNS SINGULAR	ANIMATE NOUNS PLURAL
Masculine Accusative = Genitive	Masculine Accusative = Genitive
Это стол нашего врач**а**. (Genitive) This is our doctor's table. Я вижу нашего врач**а**. (Accusative) I see our doctor.	Смотри на этих попуга**ев**! Какие милые! Look at these parrots! How cute they are!
Feminine Nouns that end with "ь" = Nominative Мы уважаем Вашу доч**ь**. We respect your daughter. **"a" is replaced with "y" "я" is replaced with "ю"** Я помню твою подруг**у**/тёт**ю**. I remember your friend/aunt.	Feminine Accusative = Genitive Я не люблю кош**ек**! Я предпочитаю соба**к**. I don't like cats! I prefer dogs.
Neutral animate nouns barely exist in the Russian language.	

ACCUSATIVE CASE FOR INANIMATE OBJECTS

INANIMATE OBJECTS SINGULAR	INANIMATE OBJECTS PLURAL
Masculine **Accusative = Nominative** **Пульт** лежит на столе. (Nominative) **The remote** control is on the table. Я вижу **пульт**. (Accusative) I see the **remote control**.	**Accusative = Nominative Plural** **for all genders** Эти красные **цветы** красивые. (Nominative) These red **flowers** are beautiful. Мне нравятся эти **цветы**. (Accusative) I like these **flowers**. **Моря** красивые. (Nominative) **Seas** are beautiful. Я рисую **моря**. (Accusative) I'm painting **seas**.
Feminine Nouns that end with "ь" = Nominative Я обожаю ноч**ь**! Волшебное время! I love the night! It's a magical time! **"а" is replaced with "у"** **"я" is replaced with "ю"** Я читаю эту книг**у**. I'm reading this book. Я в первый раз вижу такую бур**ю**! It's the first time I've seen such a storm!	
Neutral **Accusative = Nominative** **Окно** грязное. (Nominative) The window is dirty. Я мою **окно**. (Accusative) I'm washing the window.	

Note that all exceptions, peculiarities, and irregular forms that belong to the genitive case are applicable for the coinciding accusative forms.

ТВОРИТЕЛЬНЫЙ ПАДЕЖ – INSTRUMENTAL CASE

Nouns are used in the instrumental case in the following situations:

1. **To indicate the instrument, with the help of which an action is performed**

   Я режу огурцы **ножом**. – I'm cutting cucumbers with a **knife**.
   Она пишет **карандашом**. – She's writing with a **pencil**.

2. **After the preposition "с" in the meaning of "together with"**

   Я иду в кино с **друзьями**. – I'm going to the cinema **with friends**.

   Note that preposition "с" can be translated as "from," which then requires the genitive case.

   Убери вазу **с полки**. – Take the vase away **from the shelf.**

3. **After the following prepositions of place:**

   над – over, above
   под – under
   перед – in front of
   за – behind
   между – between, among

   Школа находится между **больницей** и **универмагом**.
   The school is situated between **the hospital** and **the department store**.

    Note that some prepositions may have the same translation but imply either direction or location, which influences the choice of the case.

   Я положил ключи под коврик. – I put the keys under the rug.
   "под" implies direction, so "коврик" is in the accusative case.

   Ключи под ковриком. – The keys are under the rug.
   "под" implies location, so "коврик" is in the instrumental case.

4. After the following verbs:

быть – to be
стать – become
работать – to work as
заниматься – to do, practice something
интересоваться – to be interested in

пользоваться – to use
гордиться – to be proud of
оказаться – to turn out to be
пахнуть – to smell of

Он оказался плохим **человеком**. – He turned out to be a bad **man**.
Моя дочь занимается **танцами**. – My daughter practices **dancing**.

 Remember that in the Russian language the verb "быть – to be" is omitted in the present tense, so it's only followed by a noun in the instrumental case when the verb is in the past or in the future tense form.

Она врач. – She is a doctor.
Она была врачом. – She was a doctor.
Она будет врачом. – She will be a doctor.

5. To indicate the doer of the action in the passive voice

In English, you would use the preposition "by" for the purpose, while in Russian there is no preposition needed, the noun in the instrumental case is enough.

Завод был куплен богатым **бизнесменом**.
The factory was bought **by** a rich **businessman**.

6. In time expressions to indicate:

a) The part of the day

утром – in the morning
днём – in the afternoon
вечером – in the evening
ночью – at night

b) The season

зимой – in winter
весной – in spring
летом – in summer
осенью – in autumn

Вечером я хожу на прогулку. – I go for a walk **in the evening**.
Весной у меня много энергии. – I have plenty of energy **in spring**.

THE SINGULAR FORM OF THE INSTRUMENTAL CASE

GENDER	ENDING CHANGES	EXAMPLES
Masculine	Consonant – cons. + "ом"	Бра**т** – Brother Я еду на экскурсию с брат**ом**. I'm going on an excursion with my brother.
	"й" turns into "ем"	Геро**й** – Character Я интересуюсь геро**ем** этого рассказа. I'm interested in this story's character.
	"ь" turns into "ем"	Строител**ь** – Builder Мой племянник работает строител**ем**. My nephew works as a builder.
Feminine	"a" turns into "ой"	Сестр**а** – Sister Я горжусь своей сестр**ой**. I'm proud of my sister.
	"я" turns into "ей"	Недел**я** – Week Я не доволен этой недел**ей**. I'm not happy with this week.
	"ь" + "ю"	Ноч**ь** – Night Мы выезжаем ноч**ью**. We're leaving at night.
Neutral	"о" + "м"	Лиц**о** – Face Что с твоим лиц**ом**? What is with your face?
	"е" + "м"	Солнц**е** – The sun Я наслаждаюсь солнц**ем**. I'm enjoying the sun.
	"я" turns into "енем"	Им**я** – Name Я горжусь своим им**енем**. I'm proud of my name.

IRREGULAR INSTRUMENTAL

мат**ь** – матер**ью** (mother)   доч**ь** – дочер**ью** (daughter)

Note that, according to the rules, consonants **ж, ч, ш, and щ** cannot be followed by an unstressed vowel **"о"**. In case it should be there, according to the table, replace it with **"е"**.

Example:

Я иду на вечеринку вместе с муж**ем**. – I'm going to the party with my husband.

THE PLURAL FORM OF THE INSTRUMENTAL CASE

GENDER	ENDING CHANGES	EXAMPLES
Masculine Feminine Neutral	Consonant + "ами"	Сто**л** – Table Что вы делаете с этими стол**ами**? What are you doing with these tables?
	"a" turns into "ами"	Бабушк**а** – Grandmother Мы идём гулять с бабушк**ами**. We're going for a walk with our grandmothers.
	"o" turns into "ами"	Письм**о** – Letter Займись этими письм**ами**. Их слишком много. Deal with these letters. There are too many of them.
	"й" turns into "ями"	Геро**й** – Hero Мы гордимся нашими геро**ями**. We're proud of our heroes.
	"ь" turns into "ями"	Двер**ь** – Door Что за этими двер**ями**? What is behind these doors?
	"e" turns into "ями"	Пол**е** – Field У него есть земли с большими пол**ями**. He has land with big fields.
	"я" turns into "ями"	Нян**я** – Babysitter Нам не везёт с нян**ями**. We're not lucky with babysitters.

Note that instrumental plural forms don't depend on the gender of the noun. Instead, they depend on the ending of the noun in the nominative singular.

IRREGULAR INSTRUMENTAL PLURAL

люди – люд**ьми** (people)

ПРЕДЛОЖНЫЙ ПАДЕЖ – PREPOSITIONAL CASE

As its name implies, the prepositional case is used after prepositions, such as:

на – on, at, by (the last for the means of transport)
в – in
о (об, обо) – about

Pay attention that **"на"** and **"в"** should be the prepositions of place because when they indicate direction, the accusative case should be used instead:

Я иду **на** работ**у.** – I'm going to work. (direction)
Я уже на работ**е.** – I'm already at work. (place)

 Pay attention that the preposition **"о"** can change into **"об"** when it"s followed by a vowel. It can also turn into "обо" when followed by a consonant cluster of **"вс," "мн,"** and **"чт."** Both changes are made for more convenient pronunciation.

Я не хочу думать **об э**той проблеме! – I don't want to think of this problem!
Вы говорите **обо мне**? – Are you talking about me?

THE SINGULAR FORM OF THE PREPOSITIONAL CASE

GENDER	ENDING CHANGES	EXAMPLES
Masculine	Consonant – cons. + "e"	Двоюродный бра**т** – Cousin Я думаю о моём двоюродном брат**е.** I'm thinking about my cousin.
	"й" turns into "e"	Геро**й** – Hero Она написала эссе об этом геро**е.** She's written an essay about this hero.
	"ь" turns into "e"	Водител**ь** – Driver Я ничего не знаю об этом водител**е.** I know nothing about this driver.

Feminine	"a" turns into "e"	Мам**а** – Mom Мы разговариваем о нашей мам**е**. We're talking about our Mom.
	"я turns into "e"	Недел**я** – Week Я не хочу даже думать об этой недел**е**! I don't want even to think about this week!
	"ь" turns into "и"	Двер**ь** – Door Зонтик стоит у двер**и**. The umbrella is at the door.
	"ия" turns into "ии"	Анастас**ия** – Anastasia Я не могу не думать об Анастас**ии**. I can't help thinking about Anastasia.
Neutral	"o" turns into "e"	Лиц**о** – Face Все эмоции у тебя на лиц**е**! You've got all your emotions expressed on your face!
	"e" remains "e"	Солнц**е** – The sun Я лежу на солнц**е**. I'm lying in the sun.
	"ие" turns into "ии"	Здан**ие** – Building Все дети сейчас в здан**ии**. All the kids are in the building now.
	"я" turns into "ени"	Врем**я** – Time Я думаю о свободном врем**ени** на этой неделе. I'm thinking about my free time this week.

IRREGULAR PREPOSITIONAL CASE

мать – мат**ери** (mother)

дочь – доч**ери** (daughter)

THE PLURAL FORM OF THE PREPOSITIONAL CASE

GENDER	ENDING CHANGES	EXAMPLE
Masculine Feminine Neutral	Consonant + "ах"	Мотоцик**л** – Motorcycle Поехали кататься на мотоцикл**ах**! Let's go ride motorcycles!
	"а" turns into "ах"	Подруг**а** – Female friend Мы говорим о наших подруг**ах**. We're talking about our friends.
	"о" turns into "ах"	Лиц**о** – Face Я рада видеть счастье на ваших лиц**ах**! I'm glad to see happiness on your faces!
	"й" turns into "ях"	Геро**й** – Hero Это книга о геро**ях** войны. This is a book about war heroes.
	"ь" turns into "ях"	Звер**ь** – Beast, animal Это история о диких звер**ях**. This is a story about wild animals.
	"е" turns into "ях"	Пол**е** – Field Цветы растут на пол**ях**. Flowers grow in the fields.
	"я" turns into "ях"	Нян**я** – Babysitter Мамы разговаривают о нян**ях**. Moms are talking about babysitters.

Note that prepositional plural forms don't depend on the gender of the noun. Instead, they depend on the ending of the noun in the nominative singular.

IRREGULAR NOUNS IN THE PLURAL FORM OF THE PREPOSITIONAL CASE

братья (brothers) – брать**ях**

друзья (friends) – друзь**ях**

сыновья (sons) – сыновь**ях**

матери (mothers) – матер**ях**

дочери (daughters) – дочер**ях**

дети (children) – дет**ях**

люди (people) – люд**ях**

DECLENSION OF NAMES

Grammatically, Russian first names are nouns, so they also change according to the six cases. While the choice of the ending mostly depends on the name's ending, there are a few peculiarities to pay attention to.

1. **Male first names that end in consonants or "й" are declined like the corresponding masculine nouns.**

   Влад – Vlad

   Девушка Влад**а** – Vlad's girlfriend

   Помочь Влад**у** – to help Vlad

   Я знаю Влад**а** – I know Vlad

   Я горжусь Влад**ом** – I'm proud of Vlad

   История о Влад**е** – a story about Vlad

   The same goes for foreign names that end in these letters.

   Джон – помочь Джон**у**

   John – to help John

   However, if a foreign name is in its diminutive form and ends in "и," then the noun is not declined.

   Джонн**и** – сын Джонн**и**

   Johnny – Johnny's son

2. **Male names that end in "а" are declined like feminine nouns.**

   Паша – позвонить Паше

   Pasha – to call Pasha

3. **Foreign male names that end in "о" are not declined.**

   Эдуард**о** – без Эдуард**о**

   Eduardo – without Eduardo

4. **Female names mostly end in "а" and "я" and are declined like similar nouns, even if they are foreign names.**

   Ол**я** – муж Оли

   Olya – Olya"s husband

   Даниэл**а** – я знаю Даниэл**у**

   Daniela – I know Daniela

5. **Foreign female names that end in a consonant or other vowel than "а" and "я" are not declined.**

   Аннет – книга об Аннет

   Annet – a book about Annet

   Руб**и** – дочь Руб**и**

   Ruby – Ruby's daughter

BEFORE YOU GO OVER TO THE EXERCISES

Now that you've learned about the meanings of all the six Russian cases and have an idea of how each is formed, it may seem too hard to master them all. While it's not easy, there is a way to make the challenge less tough.

First, take your time with the exercises. Initially, they will be focused on each case individually and then will become more difficult.

Second, we suggest you make use of the tables below that summarize all the endings in one place, so that you don't have to flick through the pages all the time.

Last, but not least, don't try to memorize all the cases and endings. Your initial goal is to understand how things work and put this understanding into practice. For this reason, we recommend you go back to the theory section as many times as you need.

RUSSIAN CASES SUMMARY – SINGULAR

CASE	ENDINGS		
	Masculine	Feminine	Neutral
Nominative	Consonant, -й, -ь	-а, -я, -ь,	-о, -е, -я
Genitive	-а, -я	-ы, -и, -ии	-а, -я, -ени
Dative	-у, -ю	-е, -ии, -и	-и, -у, -ю, -ени
Accusative Animate	-а, -я	-у, -ю	Accusative = Nominative
Accusative Inanimate	Accusative = Nominative	-у, -ю	Accusative = Nominative
Instrumental	-ом, -ем	-ой, -ей, ь+ю	о+м, е+м, -енем
Prepositional	Consonant + е, -е	-е, -ии, -и	-е, -и, -ени

CASE	ENDINGS		
	Masculine	**Feminine**	**Neutral**
Nominative	-ы, -и	-ы, -и, -ии	-а, -я, -ия
Genitive	Consonant + ов, -ей, -ев	-a removed, -ь, -ий, -ей	-o removed, -ий, -ей
Dative	-ам, -ям		
Accusative Animate	Consonant + ов, -ев, -ей	Accusative = Genitive	Accusative = Nominative
Accusative Inanimate	Accusative = Nominative	Accusative = Nominative	Accusative = Nominative
Instrumental	-ами, -ями		
Prepositional	-ах, -ях		

EXERCISES

1. Match the sentences with the images. Identify the noun in the genitive case.

( ) **1.** Я выпил молока.

( ) **2.** Это тетрадь моего одноклассника.

( ) **3.** Я хочу мотоцикл вместо машины.

( ) **4.** У меня три вопроса.

( ) **5.** Она купила коробку печенья.

( ) **6.** У вас нет собаки?

( ) **7.** В этом магазине мало игрушек.

( ) **8.** У Саши новый велосипед.

A.

E.

B.

F.

C.

G.

D.

H.

2. Match the sentences with the rule that explains the usage of the genitive case.

( ) **1.** Не иди на улицу без **шапки**! Don't go outside without your hat!	**A.** After the negation word "не"
( ) **2.** Сколько **гостей** ты пригласил? How many guests did you invite?	**B.** After a numeral
( ) **3.** У меня больше нет **терпения**! I don't have any more patience!	**C.** Possession
( ) **4.** Она посетила уже пять **врачей**. She's visited five doctors already.	**D.** A preposition from the list
( ) **5.** Жена твоего **друга** такая красивая! Your friend's wife is so beautiful!	**E.** Measure word
( ) **6.** У этого **чемодана** есть колёсики? Does this suitcase have wheels?	**F.** "у + есть" pattern
( ) **7.** Это уже твой третий бокал **пива**. It's your third glass of beer already.	**G.** A quantity word
( ) **8.** Можно мне **воды**? May I have some water?	**H.** Liquid quantity

3. Choose the genitive form of the noun to complete the sentences.

1. Этот подарок – сюрприз для моего _____.
   This present is a surprise for my brother.

   A. брату   **B.** брата   **C.** брате

2. Мой дом напротив _____.
   My house is opposite the church.

   A. церковь   **B.** церковью   **C.** церкви

3. На этой фотографии нет твоего _____.
   There is no face of yours in the photo.

   A. лица   **B.** лицу   **C.** лице

4. Это пальто моей _____.
   This is my mother's coat.

   A. матерью   **B.** матери   **C.** матерей

5. У меня не много _____.
   I don't have many friends.

   A. друзей   **B.** друзьях   **C.** друзьям

6. Может, выпьем _____?
   What about drinking some wine?

   A. вину   **B.** вине   **C.** вина

7. У моей тёти семь _____.
   My aunt has seven children.

   A. детях   **B.** детям   **C.** детей

8. Ты знаешь, что внутри этой _____?
   Do you know what is inside this bag?

   A. сумку   **B.** сумки   **C.** сумке

4. Put the nouns in brackets in the genitive case.

1. Москва – столица (Россия).
   Moscow is the capital of Russia.

   _____

2. Кто эта девушка у (окно)?
   Who is this girl by the window?

   _____

3. Пожалуйста, достаньте руки из (карманы).
   Please, take your hands out of the pockets.

   _____

4. У (Макар) есть свободное время для встречи?
   Does Makar have any free time for the meeting?

   _____

5. Три чашки (чай) – это слишком много для меня.
   Three cups of tea are too much for me.

   _____

6. Пришли все, кроме наших (мужья).
   Everyone except our husbands has come.

   _____

7. Мужчина, который стоит около моих (дочери), их дядя.
   The man who's standing near my daughters is their uncle.

   _____

8. У тебя два (словарь)? Можешь дать мне один?
   Have you got two dictionaries? Can you give me one?

   _____

9. Он вошёл в комнату после (жена).
   He entered the room after his wife.

   _____

10. В этом районе нет футбольного (поле).
    There is no football field in this district.

    _____

11. Хочешь (шампанское)?
    Would you like some champagne?

    _____

12. Я не пойду на вечеринку без этого (платье)!
    I'm not going to the party without this dress!

    _____

5. Listen to the sentences and fill in the missing nouns in the dative case. (Find audio on page 3.)

1. Это лекция по _____.

   This is a lecture on **chemistry**.

2. Я помогаю _____ в саду.

   I'm helping **Mom** in the garden.

3. Нашему _____ сегодня сорок пять.

   Our **boss** is forty-five today.

4. Мама сегодня идёт к _____.

   Mom is going to her **friend's** today.

5. _____ не нравятся креветки.

   Katya doesn't like shrimp.

6. Передай _____ мои поздравления.

   Send my congratulations to your **aunt**.

7. Посмотри! _____ страшно!

   Look! The **puppy** is scared.

8. Она может часами разговаривать по _____!

   She can talk on the **phone** for hours!

9. Давайте поможем этому _____.

   Let's help this **retired man**.

10. _____ нужно успеть на работу вовремя.

    Maksim needs to make it for work on time.

6. The images with the sentences below illustrate the rules for using the dative case. Match them accordingly.

( ) **1.** Talking about age

( ) **2.** Expressing likes/dislikes

( ) **3.** Preposition "по", meaning "along"

( ) **4.** After the verb "звонить"

( ) **5.** After the preposition "к", meaning "to"

( ) **6.** Expressing need for something

( ) **7.** Talking about emotions

( ) **8.** After the preposition "по", meaning by means of something

A.

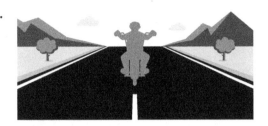

Мотоцикл едет по дороге.

E.

Мальчику грустно.

B.

Девочке нужно купить новые ботинки.

F.

Моему другу нравится мороженое.

C.

Моему сыну три года.

G.

Я звоню сестре.

D.

Бабушка и внуки разговаривают по скайпу.

H.

Малыш бежит к маме.

7. Use the correct form of the dative case to complete the sentences.

1. Врач посоветовал моей (прабабушка) хорошее лекарство.
   _____
   The doctor recommended to my great-grandmother a good medicine.

2. Этому (телеведущий) пятьдесят лет, но он молодо выглядит.
   _____
   This TV presenter is fifty but he looks young.

3. (Дети) скучно без телевизора.
   _____
   The kids are bored without the TV.

4. Я дала (племянник) свой планшет. Надеюсь, он его не сломает.
   _____
   I gave my nephew my tablet. I hope he doesn't break it.

5. Мамочки! Что это ползёт по (стена)?
   _____
   Oh dear! What is crawling on the wall?

6. Профессор пожелала (студенты) найти хорошую работу.
   _____
   The professor wished the students to find a good job.

7. Я боюсь путешествовать по (море).
   _____
   I'm afraid of travelling by sea.

8. Завтра утром я иду к своему (парикмахер).
   _____
   I'm going to my hairdresser tomorrow.

9. Моим (коллеги) не нравится новый начальник.
   _____
   My colleagues don't like our new boss.

10. Моему (друг) нужно проводить больше времени с семьёй.
    _____
    My friend needs to spend more time with his family.

8. In the sentences below, the nouns in bold are used in the accusative case because they are preceded by certain verbs. Underline these verbs.

1. О! Я <u>знаю</u> эту **песню**!

2. Девушка <u>забыла</u> **зонтик** дома.

3. Я просто <u>ненавижу</u> **крыс**. Они отвратительные!

4. Как я рада <u>видеть</u> своих дорогих **племянников**!

5. Мой дедушка до сих пор <u>любит</u> **бабушку**.

6. Ты <u>помнишь</u> про наше **свидание** завтра?

7. Дети <u>слышали</u> эту **историю** много раз.

8. Степан не <u>любит</u> **футбол**.

9. The accusative case is used after a number of prepositions. Complete the sentences with the right prepositions and pay attention to the forms of the nouns.

1. **Скорее! Спрячь книгу _____ подушку!**
   Quick! Hide the book under the pillow!

2. **Я ничего не знала _____ Аню и Кирилла. Неужели они вместе?**
   I didn't know anything about Anya and Kirill. Are they really together?

3. **Поставь вазу _____ стол.**
   Put the vase on the table.

4. **Нам пришлось идти _____ лес.**
   We had to go through the forest.

5. **Она положила деньги _____ кошелёк.**
   She put the money into the wallet.

6. **Он убрал руки _____ спину.**
   He put his arms behind his back.

10. Half of the sentences below have correct forms of accusative case, while the other half doesn't. Mark the sentences as correct/incorrect and fix the mistakes.

1. Я не могу поверить, что вижу твоё **лицу**.
   I can't believe I see your face.

   (　) incorrect　　　　(　) correct　　　　_____

2. Расскажи мне больше про своё **путешествию**.
   Tell me more about your trip.

   (　) incorrect　　　　(　) correct　　　　_____

3. Я знаю эту **актрису**.
   I know this actress.

   (　) incorrect　　　　(　) correct　　　　_____

4. Кто положил пирожное под **скатертью**?
   Who put the cake under the tablecloth?

   (　) incorrect　　　　(　) correct　　　　_____

5. Налей, пожалуйста, воду в **стакан**.
   Please, pour some water into the glass.

   (　) incorrect　　　　(　) correct　　　　_____

6. Давай повесим эту картину на **стену**!
   Let's hang this picture on the wall!

   (　) incorrect　　　　(　) correct　　　　_____

11. The sentences below have nouns in the instrumental case. Underline them and match the sentences with the corresponding rules.

( ) 1. Женщина стоит перед зеркалом. A woman is standing in front of the mirror.	**A.** After the verb "работать"
( ) 2. Я иду на реку с друзьями. I'm going to the river with friends.	**B.** To indicate the doer of the action in the passive voice
( ) 3. Мой дядя работает водителем. My uncle works as a driver.	**C.** Time expression, the season
( ) 4. Этот город был основан древним королём. This city was founded by an ancient king.	**D.** A preposition of place
( ) 5. Зимой мы часто катаемся на лыжах. We often go skiing in winter.	**E.** Time expression, part of the day
( ) 6. Перемешай салат ложкой. Mix the salad with a spoon.	**F.** After the verb "гордиться"
( ) 7. Утром они пойдут в поход. They will go hiking in the morning.	**G.** Preposition "с," meaning "together with"
( ) 8. Учитель гордится своими учениками. The teacher is proud of his pupils.	**H.** To indicate the tool

12. The images below illustrate prepositions of place that require instrumental case. Consult the theory section if necessary and write down these prepositions.

1. _____

3. _____

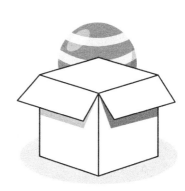

2. _____

4. _____

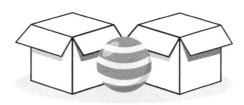

5. _____

13. Choose the right word to complete the sentences and use it in the instrumental case.

1. **Я умываю лицо _____.**
   I wash my face with water.

   A. мыло   **B.** вода   **C.** чай

2. **Когда я вырасту, я хочу стать _____.**
   When I grow up, I want to become a vet.

   A. ветеринар   **B.** строитель   **C.** юрист

3. **Совы не спят _____.**
   Owls don't sleep at night.

   A. ночь   **B.** день   **C.** утро

4. **Мне нужна лампа над _____.**
   I need a lamp above the sink.

   A. стол   **B.** кровать   **C.** раковина

5. **Он был отличным _____.**
   He was an excellent musician.

   A. актёр   **B.** мастер   **C.** музыкант

6. **Мы идём на концерт с _____.**
   We're going to the concert with my parents.

   A. родители   **B.** друзья   **C.** дети

7. **Его нога застряла между _____.**
   His leg got stuck between the rocks.

   A. стулья   **B.** камни   **C.** двери

8. **Эта книга была написана талантливым _____.**
   This book was written by a talented author.

   A. писатель   **B.** человек   **C.** автор

14. Identify which meaning the prepositions imply – direction or location – and choose the correct form of the noun, either accusative or instrumental case.

1. **Девочка пряталась под (кровать/кроватью).**
   The girl was hiding under the bed.

   ( ) direction   ( ) location

2. **Поставь подарок под (кровать/кроватью). Его никто не найдёт.**
   Put the present under the bed. No one will find it.

   ( ) direction   ( ) location

3. **Наша ферма вон там, за (холм/холмом).**
   Our farm is over there, behind the hill.

   ( ) direction   ( ) location

4. **Стая овец убежала за (холм/холмом).**
   The herd of sheep ran away behind the hill.

   ( ) direction   ( ) location

5. **Я нашёл монетку под (шкаф/шкафом).**
   I found a coin under the closet.

   ( ) direction   ( ) location

6. **Я видела мышь вон за теми (коробки/коробками)!**
   I've seen a mouse behind those boxes!

   ( ) direction   ( ) location

7. **Монетка закатилась под (шкаф/шкафом).**
   The coin rolled under the closet.

   ( ) direction   ( ) location

8. **Посылку поставили за старыми (коробки/коробками) и её потеряли.**
   The parcel was placed behind the old boxes and it was lost.

   ( ) direction   ( ) location

15. Put the nouns in brackets in the prepositional case. Remember that **"в"** and **"на"** are prepositions of place in these cases.

1. О нет! У меня оса в (волосы)! _____

2. Птицы свили гнездо на нашей (крыша). _____

3. Это история о (приключения) в джунглях. _____

4. У тебя грязь на (лицо). _____

5. Ей приснился сон об (ураган). _____

6. Я купила эти джинсы в (магазин) секонд-хенд. _____

16. Choose either accusative or prepositional case, depending on the meaning of the preposition.

1. **В этой (кашу/каше) куча комочков!**
   There are lots of lumps in this porridge!

2. **Переведи мне деньги на (карточку/карточке), пожалуйста.**
   Transfer the money to my card please.

3. **Что это за пятно у меня на (штаны/штанах)?**
   What kind of stain is this on my pants?

4. **У меня нет денег на (карточку/карточке).**
   I've got no money on my card.

5. **Тебе добавить варенья в (кашу/каше)?**
   Should I add some jam to your porridge?

6. **Я хожу в (школу/школе) пешком.**
   I go to school on foot.

7. **Посмотри на свои (штаны/штанах)! Они все мокрые!**
   Look at your pants! They're all wet!

8. **Мне не нравится в этой (школу/школе).**
   I don't like it at this school.

MISCELLANEOUS PRACTICE - NOUNS

1. Use the correct form of the noun depending on the preposition, then make the nouns plural and do the same. Remember that some nouns are always singular or always plural.

Example: с – сахар – with sugar
с сахаром (no plural form)

1. без – имя – without a name

_____

2. после – урок – after the lesson

_____

3. о – чувство – about the feeling

_____

4. внутри – игрушка – inside of the toy

_____

5. с – молоко – with milk

_____

6. о - герой - about the hero

_____

7. в – игра – in the game

_____

8. к – светофор – to the traffic lights

_____

9. на – мотоцикл – by motorcycle

_____

10. через – ворота – through the gates

_____

11. на – концерт – to the concert

_____

12. с – вершина – from the peak

_____

2. Listen to the sentences and fill in the word combinations from Exercise 1. In case you want to challenge yourself, fill in the words first and then use the audio to check. (Find audio on page 3.)

1. Иди _____. Я жду тебя там.

2. Я предпочитаю кофе _____.

3. Дети хотят знать, что находится _____.

4. Эти щенки ещё _____. Как мы их назовём?

5. Встретимся после _____?

6. Мой друг боится кататься _____.

7. У меня есть билеты_____!

8. Как мне рассказать ей _____, которые я испытываю?

9. _____ можно увидеть всю долину.

10. Я не люблю рекламу _____.

11. Сколько можно разговаривать _____?

12. Мы попали во двор _____.

3. Choose the correct case of the noun.

1. Я иду на вечеринку с _____.
   I'm going to the party with my friend.

   A. друга   **B.** другом   **C.** друге   **D.** другу

2. Он не может плавать без _____.
   He can't swim without his goggles.

   A. очков   **B.** очками   **C.** очках   **D.** очки

3. Вчера вечером она позвонила _____.
   She called her brother yesterday night.

   A. братом   **B.** брате   **C.** брата   **D.** брату

4. Что ты знаешь об этой _____?
   What do you know about this painting?

   A. картине   **B.** картиной   **C.** картинами   **D.** картина

5. У меня нет _____. Я единственный ребёнок в семье.
   I don't have a sister. I'm an only child in the family.

   A. сестры   **B.** сестру   **C.** сестрой   **D.** сестре

6. Моя бабушка очень гордится своими _____.
   My grandmother is very proud of her grandsons.

   A. внукам   **B.** внуках   **C.** внуками   **D.** внуков

7. Это дом моего _____.
   This is my neighbor's house.

   A. соседом   **B.** соседе   **C.** соседу   **D.** соседа

8. Мой сын хочет стать _____.
   My son wants to become an astronaut.

   A. космонавта   **B.** космонавтом   **C.** космонавту   **D.** космонавте

4. Fill in the gaps. Each conversation is focused on one word in different case forms. Then check, listen, and role-play the conversations. (Find audio on page 3.)

CONVERSATION 1
(БРАТ – BROTHER)

A: Я давно не видела твоего _____. Где он?

B: Ты не знала? Андрей уехал в Германию. У него новая работа.

A: Здорово! Я всегда была высокого мнения о твоём _____.

B: Спасибо! Я его просто обожаю!

A: Конечно, ты будешь скучать по _____.

B: О да! Мы с _____ всё делали вместе.

A: I haven't seen your brother for a long time. Where is he?

B: Didn't you know? Andrey has left for Germany. He's got a new job.

A: Great! I've always been of a high opinion about your brother.

B: Thank you! I just love him!

A: You will miss your brother of course.

B: Oh, I will! My brother and I used to do everything together.

 ## CONVERSATION 2
(ДЕТИ – CHILDREN)

A: Вы едете в отпуск с _____ или одни?

B: Отпуск без _____? Нет. Мы всегда проводим отпуск вместе.

A: Но _____ нужно много внимания и времени. Вы не отдохнёте!

B: О, не волнуйся о _____! Мы команда, и нам совсем не сложно вместе.

A: Что ж, тебе виднее! Хорошего вам отпуска!

A: Do you go on a holiday with the kids or alone?

B: A holiday without the kids? No. We always spend the holidays together.

A: But kids need a lot of attention and time. You won't have proper rest!

B: Oh, don't worry about the kids! We're a team and it's not hard at all for us to be together.

A: Well, you know best! Have a nice holiday!

CONVERSATION 3
(КОШКА – THE CAT)

A: Посмотри на эту _____! Она такая милая!

B: Да, милашка! А у меня нет _____.

A: Почему?

B: Мама не разрешает мне. А я так хочу иметь _____!

A: Бедняжка! Жизнь без _____ не жизнь!

B: Похоже, она голодная. Может быть, нужно дать _____ немного еды?

A: О, я знаю всё о _____! Давай пойдём в магазин и купим корм для

этой милой _____.

A: Look at this cat! She's so cute!

B: Yeah, a cutie! And I don't have a cat.

A: Why?

B: My Mom won't allow me. And I want a cat so much!

A: Poor you! A life without a cat is not a life!

B: Looks like she's hungry. Maybe we should give this cat some food?

A: Oh, I know everything about cats! Let's go to the shop and buy some food for this cute cat.

CHAPTER

2

PRONOUNS

There are several types of pronouns in the Russian language. Before we advance to studying the grammatical peculiarities of each, let's define what a pronoun is.

A pronoun is a substitute word used to define a noun without naming it directly.

While memorizing the meaning of pronouns, e.g., their translations into English, is quite easy, using them in correct grammatical forms is what causes major difficulties for Russian language learners, as pronouns change according to gender, number, and cases, with the last category being the trickiest one.

However, we don't mean to intimidate you. Instead, we want to emphasize that this book is intended to make complex things understandable and "digestible."

PART I
PERSONAL PRONOUNS

NUMBER AND GENDER

я, ты, вы (polite), он, она, оно	singular
вы, мы, они	plural
он	masculine
она	feminine
оно	neutral

 The difference between the Russian **"оно"** and the English **"it"**. While, in English, "it" is used to denote inanimate objects and animals, in Russian "оно" replaces nouns of the neutral gender (the ones that end in **"о," "е,"** and **"я"**).

Example when "it" and "оно" coincide:

The sea is beautiful today. **It** is calm and blue.
Море сегодня красивое. **Оно** спокойное и голубое.

Example when "it" and "оно" don't coincide:

This is a cat. **It** is cute and fluffy.
Это кошка. **Она** милая и пушистая.

 THE DIFFERENCE BETWEEN "ТЫ" AND "ВЫ"

Unlike in English, there are two ways in Russian for saying "you". "Ты" is informal and is used when addressing friends and good acquaintances.

"Вы" is formal and is used when we speak to:

    a. Older people;

    b. Same age people if you don't know each other*;

    c. Bosses and clients;

    d. Older relatives**;

Example:

Ты сегодня занята? – Are you busy today? (asking a friend)
Вы можете помочь мне выбрать размер? – Can you help me choose the size? (asking a shop assistant)

*It's typical to use "Вы" with all unfamiliar people (like bank workers, passers-by, shop assistants, taxi or bus drivers, receptionists, etc.) and with people you are introduced to for the first time.

**Children are supposed to use the formal way, addressing all adults outside their family and sometimes including some family members like aunts, uncles, or their parents friends. However, in this situation, much depends on the relationship. For example, in some families, nephews use the informal way to address their uncles, while in others they would say "Вы".

CASES

When it comes to Russian cases, there are two key points to pay attention to:

    1. which forms are used for certain cases

    2. in what situations certain cases are used

Let's address the first point with this brief table:

CASE FORMS OF PERSONAL PRONOUNS

NOMINATIVE	GENITIVE	DATIVE	ACCUSATIVE	INSTRUMENTAL	PREPOSITIONAL
я – I	меня	мне	меня	мной	мне
ты – you	тебя	тебе	тебя	тобой	тебе
мы – we	нас	нам	нас	нами	нас
вы – you	вас	вам	вас	вами	вас
он – he	его	ему	его	им	нём
она – she	её	ей	её	ею	ней
оно – it	его	ему	его	им	нём
они – they	их	им	их	ими	них

Now let's go to the second point and see when you should use this or that form.

NOMINATIVE CASE

The nominative case is the initial form that is used when a pronoun is the subject of the sentence.

Она работает в большой корпорации. – **She** works in a big corporation.
Мы не придём на вечеринку. – **We**'re not coming to the party.

GENITIVE CASE

Pronouns in the genitive case are used in the following situations:

1. **In negative sentences that denote the absence of the person/object that the pronoun defines;**

   Мои родители уехали в отпуск. **Их нет** дома.
   My parents have left for a vacation. **They** are **not** at home.

2. **After the following prepositions:**

без – without	вокруг – around
для – for	напротив – opposite
кроме – except	до – before
вместо – instead of	после – after

   Никто, **кроме тебя**, не пришёл. – No one came **except you**.
   Я купил эти цветы **для неё**. – I've bought these flowers **for her**.

3. **In the following patterns:**

У + pronoun in genitive + есть

У + pronoun in genitive + нет

У нас есть несколько вопросов. – **We have** a few questions.
У Вас нет денег на счету. – **You have** no money on your account.

DATIVE CASE

Pronouns in the dative case are used in the following situations:

1. **When pronouns indicate an indirect object – a person or object to whom the action is done;**

    Маша отдала **ему** книгу. – Masha gave the book **to him.**
    Я звоню **им**. – I'm calling **them.**

2. **When expressing feelings and emotions – pronoun in dative + the adverb;**

    Мне холодно. – **I** am cold.
    Вам грустно? – Are **you** sad?

3. **With the preposition "к"/"ко" – "to," "toward";**

    Иди **ко мне**! – Come **to me**!

4. **With the verb "нравится" – "like";**

    Мне нравится вишнёвое мороженое. – **I like** cherry ice-cream.

5. **When talking about age;**

    Ему двадцать лет. – **He**'s twenty years old.
    Сколько **тебе** лет? – How old are **you**?

6. **When expressing the need for something.**

    Мне нужно купить новую куртку. – **I need** to buy a new jacket.
    Вам не нужно бронировать столик. – **You don't need** to book a table.

ACCUSATIVE CASE

Pronouns in the accusative case are used in the following situations:

1. When pronouns indicate the direct object, e.g., the object to which the action is directed straightforwardly;

   Я не знаю **Вас**. – I don't know **you**.
   Она видит **их** через окно. – She sees **them** through the window.

2. After the following prepositions:

   в – to, into (direction)   за – behind (direction)
   на – on, onto (direction)   про – about
   под – under (direction)   через – through

   Вы не забыли **про меня**? – Have you forgotten **about me**?

INSTRUMENTAL CASE

Pronouns in the instrumental case are used after the following prepositions:

   с – with   перед – in front of
   над – above   за – behind (place)
   под – under (place)   между - between

   Ты идёшь **с нами**? – Are you coming **with us**?
   Я не хочу сидеть **между вами**! – I don't want to sit **between you**!

 Pay attention to the difference between the prepositions of direction and place.

Compare:

Это стол. Поставь коробку **под него**. – It's a table. Place the box **under it**.
"Под" here is a preposition of direction, so we use the accusative case.

Это стол. Коробка **под ним**. – It's a table. The box is **under it**.
"Под" here is a preposition of place, so we use the instrumental case.

PREPOSITIONAL CASE

Pronouns in the prepositional case are used after the following prepositions:

о – about
в – in (place)
на – on (place)

Я ничего **о вас** не знаю. – I know nothing **about you**.
Видишь стакан? Налей **в него** воду. – Do you see the glass? Pour some water into it.

 Make sure to pay attention to the difference between the prepositions of place and direction, like in the situation described above.

 Pay attention to spelling rules:

a. Prepositions **"к"**, **"с"**, and **"о"** turn into **"ко"**, **"со"**, and **"обо"** when followed by the forms of the pronoun **"я"**;

Вы слышали **обо мне**? – Have you heard **about me**?
Ты придёшь **ко мне**? – Will you come **to me**?
Поиграй **со мной**! – Play **with me**!

b. The forms of **"она"**, **"он"**, and **"они"** take an **"н"** at the beginning in all cases except nominative, when preceded by a preposition.

Пойдём **к нему**! – Let's go **to him**!
Эти подарки **для неё**. – These presents are **for her**.
Я не хочу выбирать **между ними**. – I don't want to choose **between them**.

EXERCISES

1. Match the nouns with the images and replace them with the corresponding pronouns.

( ) **1.** девочка

( ) **2.** соседи

( ) **3.** молоко

( ) **4.** мой брат и я

( ) **5.** мужчина

( ) **6.** кошка

( ) **7.** ты и твои коллеги

( ) **8.** море

A. _____

B. _____

C. _____

D. _____

E. _____

F. _____

G. _____

H. _____

2. Choose the correct pronoun.

1. Это Ангелина. _____ моя сестра.

    A. оно

    B. она

    C. он

2. Это Саша и Антон. _____ друзья.

    A. вы

    B. он

    C. они

3. Александр Петрович, _____ свободны сегодня?

    A. Вы

    B. он

    C. вы

4. Это наш дом. _____ новый.

    A. оно

    B. он

    C. она

5. Это яйцо плохо пахнет. _____ испорченное.

    A. он

    B. она

    C. оно

6. Макар и я учимся в одном классе. _____ одноклассники.

    A. вы

    B. мы

    C. они

3. Choose the correct case form of the pronoun.

1. **Мы пойдём на пляж с (тобой/тебя).**

    We're going to the beach with you.

2. **Что это висит на стене? (Мне/Мной) страшно!**

    What is hanging on the wall? I'm scared!

3. **Откуда вы знаете (нам/нас)?**

    How do you know us?

4. **Этот кусок пирога для (ему/него). Не ешь (он/его).**

    This piece of pie is for him. Don't eat it.

5. **Что ты знаешь о (её/ней)? Она свободна?**

    What do you know about her? Is she single?

6. **Сколько (Вам/Вас) лет?**

    How old are you?

7. **Не могли бы вы помочь (них/им) с бумагами?**

    Could you help them with the papers?

8. **Извините, у (мной/меня) совсем нет времени на это.**

    I'm sorry, I have absolutely no time for it.

9. **Кто-нибудь был в комнате после (вам/вас)?**

    Has anybody been in the room after you?

10. **(Тебя/Тебе) нужна моя помощь?**

    Do you need my help?

4. Use the corresponding form of the pronoun in brackets depending on the meaning – direction or location.

A.

1. Это коробка. Подарок уже в (она).   _____
   It's a box. The present is already in it.

2. Это коробка. Положи подарок в (она).   _____
   It's a box. Put the present into it.

B.

1. Это шторы. Цветок за (они).   _____
   These are curtains. The flower is behind them.

2. Это шторы. Поставь цветок за (они).   _____
   These are curtains. Put the flower behind them.

C.

1. Это стол. Журнал на (он).   _____
   This is a table. The magazine is on it.

2. Это стол. Положи журнал на (он).   _____
   This is a table. Put the magazine on it.

D.

1. Это покрывало. Положи подушку под (оно).   _____
   This is a blanket. Put the pillow under it.

2. Это покрывало. Подушка под (оно).   _____
   This is a blanket. The pillow is under it.

5. Listen to the conversations and fill in the missing pronouns. If you want to challenge yourself, fill in the pronouns yourself and check if correct with the audio.

CONVERSATION I

A: Привет, Антон! У меня есть просьба к **1)** _____.

B: Привет, Катя! Конечно! Что **2)** _____ нужно?

A: Ты можешь выйти на работу завтра вместо **3)** _____?

B: Извини, я хочу помочь **4)** _____, но я тоже занят завтра.

A: Как жаль!

B: А ты просила кого-нибудь, кроме **5)** _____?

A: Ещё нет.

B: Позвони Марине. **6)** _____ может помочь.

A: Точно! Позвоню **7)** _____! Спасибо! Что бы я делала без **8)** _____!

A: Hi Anton! I have something to ask you.

B: Hi Katya! Sure! What do you need?

A: Can you come to work tomorrow instead of me?

B: Sorry, I want to help you but I'm busy tomorrow as well.

A: What a pity!

B: Have you asked anyone besides me?

A: Not yet.

B: Call Marina. She may help.

A: Exactly! I'll call her! Thank you! What would I do without you!

A: Посмотри на эту собаку! **1)** _____, наверное, холодно.

B: Да, **2)** _____ вся дрожит.

A: Может быть, возьмём **3)** _____ домой?

B: У **4)** _____ уже есть пять собак. Наш дом не приют.

A: Эй, отличная идея! Давай отвезём **5)** _____ в приют.

B: Точно, там **6)** _____ помогут.

A: Интересно, сколько **7)** _____ лет?

B: Не знаю, **8)** _____ выглядит старой.

A: Иди ко **9)** _____, бедняжка. Мы отвезём **10)** _____ в хорошее место.

A: Look at this dog! It must be cold.

B: Yes, it's all shivering.

A: Maybe we take it home?

B: We already have five dogs. Our house is not a shelter.

A: Hey, great idea! Let's take it to the shelter.

B: Right, they will help it there.

A: I wonder how old it is.

B: I don't know, it looks old.

A: Come to me, poor thing. We'll take you to a good place.

PART II
POSSESSIVE PRONOUNS

Just like personal pronouns, possessive pronouns change according to gender, number, and cases. The gender, number, and case of a possessive pronoun are defined by the form of the noun that denotes the object/person of possession.

Мой дом – My house

"Дом" is singular masculine nominative, so the pronoun has the same attributes.

Дом **моей сестры – My sister's** house

"Сестра" is singular, feminine, genitive, so the pronoun has the same attributes.

First, take a look at the table to see what Russian possessive pronouns look like and how they correspond with the personal ones.

PERSONAL PRONOUN	POSSESSIVE PRONOUN
я – I	мой – my
ты – you	твой – your
мы – we	наш – our
вы (Вы) – you	ваш (Ваш) – your
он – he	его – his
она – she	её – her
оно – it	его – its
они – they	их – their

Мы купили новый дом. Это **наш** дом. – **We**'ve bought a new house. It's **our** house.

 Note that possessive pronouns for **"он," "она," "оно,"** and **"они"** correspond to the forms of these personal pronouns in the accusative case and are the same for all numbers, genders, and cases, which makes things easier for you.

Я знаю **его**. – I know **him**. (Accusative)

Это **его** сын. – This is **his** son. (Possessive)

Now you're ready to go over to the grammatical forms. Let's start with the number.

POSSESSIVE PRONOUNS IN SINGULAR AND PLURAL

SINGULAR	PLURAL
мой	мои
твой	твои
наш	наши
ваш	ваши
его	их
её	их
его (neutral)	их
их	их

CASE FORMS OF POSSESSIVE PRONOUNS

GENDER NUMBER	NOMINATIVE	GENITIVE	DATIVE	ACCUSATIVE		INSTRUMENTAL	PREPOSITIONAL
				ANIM.	INANIM.		
Masculine Singular	Мой	Моего	Моему	Моего	Мой	Моим	Моём
	Твой	Твоего	Твоему	Твоего	Твой	Твоим	Твоём
	Наш	Нашего	Нашему	Нашего	Наш	Нашим	Моём
	Ваш	Вашего	Вашему	Вашего	Ваш	Вашим	Вашем
Feminine Singular	Моя	Моей	Моей	Мою		Моей	Моей
	Твоя	Твоей	Твоей	Твою		Твоей	Твоей
	Наша	Нашей	Нашей	Нашу		Нашей	Нашей
	Ваша	Вашей	Вашей	Вашу		Вашей	Вашей
Neutral Singular	Моё	Моего	Моему	Моё		Моим	Моём
	Твоё	Твоего	Твоему	Твоё		Твоим	Твоём
	Наше	Нашего	Нашему	Наше		Нашим	Моём
	Ваше	Вашего	Вашему	Ваше		Вашим	Вашем
Plural	Мои	Моих	Моим	Моих	Мои	Моими	Моих
	Твои	Твоих	Твоим	Твоих	Твои	Твоими	Твоих
	Наши	Наших	Нашим	Наших	Наши	Нашими	Наших
	Ваши	Ваших	Вашим	Ваших	Ваши	Вашими	Ваших

When choosing which case to use, be guided by the noun that the possessive pronoun defines. In other words, you first choose the case for the noun and then create the corresponding form for the pronoun.

 **EXERCISES**

1. Create word combinations according to the sample and match them with the images.

я/деньги – мои деньги

( ) **1.** ты/костюм   ( ) **5.** мы/билеты

( ) **2.** вы/подруга   ( ) **6.** Вы/документы

( ) **3.** он/шляпа   ( ) **7.** они/дети

( ) **4.** я/книга   ( ) **8.** оно/лучи

A.

E.

B.

F.

C.

G.

D.

H.

2. Match the nouns with the corresponding possessive pronouns.

( ) 1. дядя	( ) 5. архитектор	**A.** его
( ) 2. сестра	( ) 6. море	**B.** её
( ) 3. родители	( ) 7. певица	
( ) 4. птицы	( ) 8. молоко	**C.** их

3. Fill in the pronouns from Exercise 2 and see how they remain the same in different case and gender forms.

Это молоко свежее? **Его вкус** какой-то странный.
Is this milk fresh? **Its taste** is weird.

Добавь в молоко куркуму. Это придаст **его вкусу** интересный оттенок.
Add some turmeric to your milk. It will give an interesting touch to **its taste**.

1. **Он знаменитый архитектор.** _____ **здания очень красивые. Я знаю**

   много интересного о _____ **соборе.** (nominative, prepositional)

   He's a famous architect. His buildings are very beautiful. I know a lot of interesting things about his cathedral.

2. **Это редкие птицы.** _____ **гнездо у нас в саду. Интересно, нам можно**

   посмотреть на _____ **птенцов?** (nominative, accusative)

   These are rare birds. Their nest is in our garden. I wonder if we can take a look at their nestlings.

3. **Я обожаю эту певицу. Я не знаю, как бы я жила без** _____ **песен!**

   _____ **голосу нужно поставить памятник!** (genitive, dative)

   I love this singer! I don't know how I would live without her songs! One needs to put up a monument to her voice!

4. **Мой дядя бизнесмен. Я горжусь** _____ **достижениями. Я работаю в**

   _____ **компании.** (instrumental, prepositional)

   My uncle is a businessman. I'm proud of his achievements. I work at his company.

4. Choose the right possessive pronoun.

1. _____ волосы такие густые! Каким шампунем ты пользуешься?
   Your hair is so thick! What shampoo do you use?

   A. твоя   **B.** твоё   **C.** твои   **D.** твой

2. Отлично! Мне нравится _____ идея, Геннадий Петрович!
   Great! I like your idea, Gennadiy Petrovich!

   A. Ваша   **B.** Ваш   **C.** Ваше   **D.** Ваши

3. Это какая-то ошибка. Это не _____ номер телефона.
   This has to be some mistake. It's not my phone number.

   A. мой   **B.** моя   **C.** мои   **D.** моё

4. Наши дети – это _____ счастье.
   Our children are our happiness.

   A. наши   **B.** наша   **C.** наш   **D.** наше

5. Саша и Макар, это _____ игрушки?
   Sasha and Makar, are these your toys?

   A. ваши   **B.** ваша   **C.** ваш   **D.** ваше

6. Извините, но _____ магазин не работает после полуночи.
   I'm sorry, but our store doesn't work after midnight.

   A. наше   **B.** наш   **C.** наша   **D.** наши

7. _____ подруга сейчас в отпуске.
   My friend is on a holiday now.

   A. мой   **B.** мои   **C.** моя   **D.** моё

8. Извините, но это не _____ место.
   I'm sorry but it's not your seat.

   A. Ваш   **B.** Ваши   **C.** Ваша   **D.** Ваше

5. Choose the right case form of the possessive pronouns.

1. Ты уверена, что это квартира (твоей/твою) сестры?
   Are you sure this is your sister's apartment?

2. Я ничего не знаю о (вашу/вашей) проблеме.
   I don't know anything about your problem.

3. Ты знаком с (мою/моей) подругой Ниной?
   Have you met my friend Nina?

4. Могу я помочь (Ваших/Вашим) ученикам?
   Can I help your students?

5. Мы так гордимся (нашими/наших) детьми.
   We're so proud of our children!

6. Почему ты пишешь (моя/моей) ручкой? Где твоя?
   Why are you writing with my pen? Where is yours?

7. Я бы не справился без (твоих/твоими) советов!
   I wouldn't have done it without your advice!

8. Супермаркет как раз напротив (моему/моего) дома.
   The supermarket is right opposite my house.

9. Мы едем к (наших/нашим) общим родственникам.
   We're going to our common relatives.

10. Извините, но здесь нет (ваших/вашими) писем.
    I'm sorry, but your letters are not here.

11. Хочешь выпить (мой/моему) коктейль вместо меня? Эта порция слишком большая для меня.
    Would you like to drink my cocktail instead of me? This serving is too big for me.

12. (Твоего/твоему) котёнку холодно?
    Is your kitten cold?

6. Read the conversations and fill in the right forms of possessive pronouns. Then check, listen, and role-play.

CONVERSATION I

A: Маргарита Николаевна, Вы можете поговорить с **1)** _____ сыном?

B: Да, Алина, конечно. А что не так с **2)** _____ сыном?

A: Ну, Вы знаете, что я люблю Степана, он **3)** _____ муж и **4)** _____ семья просто замечательная, но он такой неряха!

B: О, Алина! Я тебя понимаю! Степан – это катастрофа **5)** _____ семьи!

6) _____ папа такой аккуратный.

A: Я рада, что Вы понимаете **7)** _____ проблему, но что мне делать? Сегодня

я нашла **8)** _____ носки под столом на кухне!

B: О, бедняжка! **9)** _____ нервам нужен отдых. Я поговорю со Степаном, обещаю.

A: Да, пожалуйста, иначе он превратит **10)** _____ дом в свалку!

A: Margarita Nikolaevna, can you talk to your son?

B: Yes, Alina, sure. And what is wrong with my son?

A: Well, you know that I love Stepan, he's my husband and our family is just great, but he's such a mess!

B: Oh, Alina! I do understand you! Stepan is the catastrophe of our family. His dad is so neat.

A: I'm glad you understand my problem but what do I do? I found his socks under the kitchen table today!

B: Oh, poor you! Your nerves need a rest. I will talk to Stepan, I promise.

A: Please do or he'll turn our house into a junk yard.

A: Здравствуйте, мы бы хотели выбрать подарок для **1)** _____ родителей. Вы не могли бы нам помочь?

B: С удовольствием! Могу я узнать больше о **2)** _____ родителях? Сколько им лет?

C: Папе пятьдесят пять, а маме... Ты помнишь возраст **3)** _____ мамы, Егор?

A: 4) _____ память просто ужасная в последнее время. Дай подумать. Маме пятьдесят один.

B: Замечательно! Какой **5)** _____ повод? Годовщина?

C: Нет. У **6)** _____ родителей день рождения в один день.

B: Какое совпадение! Что ж, давайте посмотрим, что я могу вам предложить.

A: Hi, we'd like to choose a present for our parents. Could you help us?

B: With pleasure! May I know more about your parents. How old are they?

C: Dad is fifty-five and Mom... Do you remember our Mom's age, Egor?

A: My memory has been just terrible recently. Let me think. Mom is fifty-one.

B: Great! What is their occasion? An anniversary?

C: No. Our parents have their birthdays on the same day.

B: What a coincidence! Well, let's see what I can offer you.

A: Привет, Милана! Я принесла **1)** _____ учебник по химии.

B: Привет, Даша! **2)** _____ учебник был у тебя всё это время?

A: Да, я взяла его по ошибке, извини.

B: Ничего страшного! Главное, что он у меня. Без **3)** _____ любимого учебника я не сдам экзамен.

A: Кстати, расскажи мне о **4)** _____ экзамене по физике. Как он прошёл?

B: Неплохо, но профессор недоволен результатами **5)** _____ группы.

A: Но он доволен **6)** _____ результатом?

B: Да, с **7)** _____ результатом всё в порядке.

A: Это главное!

A: Hi, Milana! I brought you your chemistry book.

B: Hi, Dasha! My textbook has been with you all this time?

A: Yes, I took it by mistake. I'm sorry.

B: That's okay! The main thing is that I have it with me. I won't pass the exam without my favorite textbook.

A: By the way, tell me about your physics exam. How did it go?

B: Not bad, but the professor is not happy with the results of our group.

A: But is he happy with your result?

B: Yes, my result is all right.

A: That's the main thing!

PART III
REFLEXIVE AND DEMONSTRATIVE PRONOUNS

REFLEXIVE PRONOUNS

Reflexive pronouns form a group of pronouns that are used to refer to a noun or a pronoun.

PRONOUN "СВОЙ"

The pronoun **"свой"** usually causes confusion with foreign Russian learners, since there is no corresponding pronoun in English as well as in many other languages.

This reflexive pronoun is used instead of a possessive pronoun when we need to refer an object to the subject of the sentence, i.e., to the doer of the action.

Example: Он любит **свой** дом. – He likes **his** house.

In this case, we use the pronoun "свой" because the object (the house) belongs to the subject (he).

However, if an object belongs to some other person or object, then we should use a regular possessive pronoun.

Example: Я иду в гости к Андрею. Это **его** дом. – I'm going to visit Andrew. This is **his** house.

With the 1st and 2nd person you can use either the pronoun "свой" or the corresponding possessive pronoun.

Example: Покажи мне **твой/свой** дом. – Show me your house.
Я крашу **мой/свой** дом. – I am painting my house.

 Remember that with the 3rd person the differentiation between the reflexive and the possessive pronoun is obligatory.

 Unlike in English, there is no need to use a possessive pronoun when talking about body parts.

Compare: Я чищу зубы. – I'm cleaning **my** teeth.

DECLENSION OF THE PRONOUN "СВОЙ" ACCORDING TO GENDER, NUMBER, AND CASE

GENDER/NUMBER	NOMINATIVE	GENITIVE	DATIVE	ACCUSATIVE	INSTRUMENTAL	PREPOSITIONAL
Masculine	свой	своего	своему	animate = genitive inanimate = nominative	своим	своём
Feminine	своя	своей	своей	свою	своей	своей
Neutral	своё	своего	своему	своё	своим	своём
Plural	свои	своих	своим	animate = genitive inanimate = nominative	своими	своих

PRONOUN "СЕБЯ"

This pronoun is used to indicate that the action performed by the subject is directed toward the subject itself. Its English equivalent is the pronoun -self.

Можете рассказать немного о **себе**? – Can you tell a bit about **yourself**?

 This pronoun doesn't depend on the gender or the number of the noun to which it refers and changes only according to cases.

THE CASE FORMS RESEMBLE THAT OF THE PRONOUN "ТЫ"

NOMINATIVE	-
GENITIVE	себя
DATIVE	себе
ACCUSATIVE	себя
INSTRUMENTAL	собой
PREPOSITIONAL	себе

Note that there are reflexive verbs in Russian that express a similar meaning and the pronoun "себя" is never used with these verbs. You will learn more about these verbs further in the book but, meanwhile, you can identify them by endings "ся" and "сь".

Не забудь **умыться**! – Don't forget to **wash yourself**!

 Reflexive pronoun "себя" is used in a range of idiomatic and set expressions:

чувствовать себя – feel

вести себя – behave

брать с собой – take (with)

представлять себе – imagine

мне не по себе – I feel uneasy

так себе – so-so

ничего себе – wow! no way!

выйти из себя – lose temper

быть собой – be yourself

у себя – at one's working place, office, home

Ты бледная! Как ты **себя чувствуешь**? – You're pale! How **do you feel**?
Я всегда **беру с собой** перекус на работу. – I always **take** a snack to work.

PRONOUN "САМ"

This pronoun indicates the fact that the subject performs the action independently without any help. In English, its initial form corresponds to "by myself."

Я нарисовал эту картину **сам**. Учитель не помогал мне.

I've painted this picture **by myself**. The teacher didn't help me.

The pronoun can also precede the verb:

Он **сам** может застелить свою кровать. – He can make his bed **by himself**.

The pronoun changes only according to number and gender:

Masculine: сам

Feminine: сама

Neutral: само

Plural: сами

PRONOUN "ДРУГ ДРУГА"

It's a reciprocal pronoun that corresponds to the English "each other/one another". The first part of the pronoun never changes, while the other is declined according to cases.

Note that when a sentence requires a preposition, it is placed between the two parts of the pronoun.

Мы часто звоним **друг другу**. – We often call each other.

Они не могут жить **друг без друга**. – They can't live **without each other**.

The table below demonstrates the declension of the pronoun with example prepositions.

NOMINATIVE	–
GENITIVE	друг друга друг от друга
DATIVE	друг другу друг к другу
ACCUSATIVE	друг друга друг про друга
INSTRUMENTAL	друг другом друг с другом
PREPOSITIONAL	not used without a preposition друг о друге

DEMONSTRATIVE PRONOUNS

Russian demonstrative pronouns are **"это"** and **"то"** and correspond to the English **"this"** and **"that"**. Both are used as noun modifiers and have to agree with the noun in gender, number and case.

Этот дом новый. – **This** house is new.
Та картина очень дорогая. – **That** painting is very expensive.

The pronoun **"этот"** is used to describe a noun that is close to the speaker or is related to the present, while **"тот"** is used for nouns that are farther in distance and are related to the past.

1. Я хочу купить **эту** книгу. – I want to buy **this** book.
2. Я хочу посмотреть на **ту** книгу. – I want to take a look at **that** book.

The pronoun "тот" is also used as the other element of an opposition.

Эта рубашка моя, а **та** моего брата. – **This** shirt is mine and **that** one is my brother's.

Pay attention to the difference between the indeclinable **"это"** and the demonstrative pronouns, as both are often confused. The former corresponds to the English **"this is"** and **"these are"**, while the latter have a descriptive character.

Это мой сад. – **This is** my garden.
Этот сад такой красивый! – **This** garden is so beautiful!

DECLENSION OF PRONOUN "ЭТОТ"

	Masculine	Feminine	Neutral	Plural
NOMINATIVE	этот	эта	это	эти
GENITIVE	этого	этой	этого	этих
DATIVE	этому	этой	этому	этим
ACCUSATIVE	animate = genitive inanimate = nominative	эту	это	animate = genitive inanimate = nominative
INSTRUMENTAL	этим	этой	этим	этими
PREPOSITIONAL	этом	этой	этом	этих

DECLENSION OF PRONOUN "TOT"

	Masculine	Feminine	Neutral	Plural
NOMINATIVE	тот	та	то	те
GENITIVE	того	той	того	тех
DATIVE	тому	той	тому	тем
ACCUSATIVE	animate = genitive inanimate = nominative	ту	то	animate = genitive inanimate = nominative
INSTRUMENTAL	тем	той	тем	теми
PREPOSITIONAL	том	той	тому	тех

EXERCISES

1. Choose between the pronoun "свой", a possessive pronoun, or its absence. When several options are possible, mark it accordingly.

1. Хочешь, я покажу тебе (свою/мою) коллекцию монет?
Would you like me to show you my collection of coins?

2. Мне кажется, Кристина слишком сильно любит (свою/её) собаку.
It seems to me that Kristina loves her dog too much.

3. Кристина и (своя/её) собака даже похожи!
Kristina and her dog even look alike!

4. Когда ты познакомишь меня с (твоими/своими) родителями?
When will you introduce me to your parents?

5. Они не любят говорить о (своих/их) проблемах.
They don't like talking about their problems.

6. Я не люблю мыть (свои/-) волосы.
I don't like washing my hair.

7. Дети, уберите (свои/ваши) игрушки.
Kids, pick up your toys.

8. Мы не можем рассказать вам о (своих/наших) секретах.
We can't tell you about our secrets.

9. Оля опаздывает. Ты сможешь отправить (свою/её) посылку?
Olya is running late. Will you be able to send her parcel?

10. Вы не любите (свою/Вашу) работу. Это видно.
You don't like your job. One can see it.

11. Она помыла (свои/-) руки и пошла на кухню.
She washed her hands and went to the kitchen.

12. Это сад Жени. Садовник убирает (свой/его) сад.
This is Zhenya's garden. The gardener is cleaning his garden.

2. Choose the correct form of the pronoun "свой".

1. Я пришёл на встречу без _____ ежедневника.
   I've come to the meeting without my planner.

   A. своему   **B.** свой   **C.** своего   **D.** своим

2. Она так гордится _____ достижениями.
   She's so proud of her achievements.

   A. своими   **B.** своих   **C.** свои   **D.** своим

3. Она хочет продать _____ старую дачу.
   She wants to sell her old country house.

   A. своя   **B.** свою   **C.** своей   **D.** своего

4. Мои родители ничего не знают про _____ бывших одноклассников.
   My parents don't know anything about their former classmates.

   A. своим   **B.** своих   **C.** своими   **D.** свои

5. Постарайся скрыть _____ раздражение.
   Try to hide your irritation.

   A. своего   **B.** своим   **C.** своими   **D.** своё

6. Можешь дать мне кусочек _____ пирога?
   Could you give me a piece of your pie?

   A. своему   **B.** свой   **C.** своего   **D.** своим

7. Ты едешь к _____ другу на вечеринку?
   Do you go to your friend's party?

   A. своему   **B.** своим   **C.** своего   **D.** свой

8. Почему ты не пользуешься _____ новой косметикой?
   Why don't you use your new cosmetics?

   A. своя   **B.** свой   **C.** свою   **D.** своей

3. Fill in the correct form of the pronoun "себя."

1. Мой дедушка часто разговаривает сам с _____.
   My grandfather often talks to himself.

2. Почему ты ненавидишь _____?
   Why do you hate yourself?

3. Если никто тебе не помогает, помоги _____ сама!
   If nobody helps you, help yourself!

4. Всё свидание он говорил только о _____.
   During all the date, he was talking only about himself.

5. Малыш увидел _____ в зеркале и засмеялся.
   The baby saw himself in the mirror and laughed.

6. Ты должна быть _____! Не притворяйся.
   You have to be yourself! Don't pretend.

4. Choose between the forms of "сам" and "себя".

1. Мы с братом (**сами/собой**) делаем домашнее задание. Мама редко помогает нам.
   My brother and I do our homework by ourselves. Mom rarely helps us.

2. Я не узнаю (**сама/себя**)! Это моя третья тренировка за неделю!
   I don't recognize myself! It's my third workout this week!

3. Она заботиться о (**сама/себе**), чтобы хорошо выглядеть.
   She cares about herself to look well.

4. Окно открылось (**само/себя**) и напугало меня до смерти.
   The window opened by itself and frightened me to death.

5. Она отправила (**сама/себе**) сообщение, чтобы не потерять его.
   She sent the message to herself so as not to lose it.

6. Это самая лучшая пицца на свете! Мой двоюродный брат (**сам/себе**) её готовит.
   It's the best pizza in the world! My cousin cooks it by himself.

5. Fill in the correct forms of the pronoun "друг друга" and match the sentences with the images.

(　　) **1.** Они пишут _____ по сто раз на дню.

(　　) **2.** Лебеди не могут жить _____ без _____.

(　　) **3.** Дети в лагере рассказали _____ о _____.

(　　) **4.** Наши собаки часто играют _____ с _____.

(　　) **5.** Мы смотрим _____ на _____ через окно.

(　　) **6.** Они были рады увидеть _____ снова.

A.

D.

B.

E.

C.

F.

6. Group the word combinations into two columns. Remember to consult a dictionary when necessary.

Это сообщение, та ошибка, тот преступник, эти макароны, эта актриса, этот роман, те спортсмены, то здание, эта юбка, то пальто, эти задания, это лекарство, тот компьютер, та история.

Close to the speaker, related to the present	Far from the speaker, related to the past

7. Fill in some of the words from Exercise 6, using them in the correct case forms.

1. Сколько лет _____ за углом?
   How old are those buildings over the corner?

2. Все говорят об _____. Это новый бестселлер.
   Everyone is talking about this novel. It's a new bestseller.

3. _____ облегчит боль в горле.
   This medicine will relieve a sore throat.

4. Суд уже решил, что сделает с _____, которого поймали в прошлом месяце?
   Has the court already decided what they'll do to that criminal they caught last month?

5. Не говори мне про _____, которую я сделала в прошлом тесте.
   Don't tell me about that mistake I made in the previous test.

6. Мой друг интересуется _____.
   My friend is interested in this actress.

7. _____ плохо? Почему они остановились?
   Are those sportsmen unwell? Why did they stop?

8. Дедушка, расскажи _____ про пиратов ещё раз!
   Grandpa, tell us that story about the pirates one more time!

8. Fill in the correct pronouns to complete the conversations. Then check, listen, and role-play.

CONVERSATION I

A: Дорогая, ты выбираешь пальто уже час. Я устал.

B: Я понимаю. Ты устал, но **1)** _____ пальто мне не нравится.

A: А **2)** _____ синее слева?

B: Я не нравлюсь **3)** _____ в синем цвете!

A: О, нет! Дорогая, я начинаю выходить из **4)** _____!

B: Ладно, жди меня в кафе. Я выберу пальто **5)** _____.

A: О, спасибо! Теперь я узнаю **6)** _____ жену!

A: Darling, you've been choosing a coat for an hour already. I'm tired.

B: I understand. You're tired but I don't like this coat.

A: And what about that one on the left?

B: I don't like myself in blue color.

A: Oh, no! Darling, I'm starting to lose my temper!

B: All right, wait for me in the café. I'll choose the coat myself.

A: Oh, thank you! Now I recognize my wife!

A: Виктор Павлович у **1)** _____?

B: Да, он в кабинете. Вы можете войти.

A: Здравствуйте, Виктор Павлович!

C: О, Андрей Семёнович! Как Вы **2)** _____ чувствуете?

A: Спасибо, намного лучше. Я уже исправил **3)** _____ неверный отчёт.

C: Замечательно!

A: Я обратил внимание на Ваши замечания.

C: Как хорошо, что мы понимаем **4)** _____!

A: Согласен с Вами.

C: Тогда я принимаю отчёт и **5)** _____ отправлю его в головной офис.

A: Is Victor Pavlovich in his office?

B: Yes, he's in the office. You can come in.

A: Hello, Victor Pavlovich!

C: Oh, Andrey Semenovich! How do you find yourself?

A: Much better, thank you! I've fixed the incorrect report already.

C: Great!

A: I paid attention to your remarks.

C: It's so good we understand each other!

A: I agree with you.

C: Then I accept the report and will send it to the head office myself.

PART IV
INTERROGATIVE AND NEGATIVE PRONOUNS

INTERROGATIVE PRONOUNS

Interrogative pronouns are used to ask questions. For your convenience, we've divided them into two groups:

1. Pronouns **"кто – who,"** **"что – what,"** and **"сколько – how many"** that change only according to cases;

2. Pronouns **"какой – what kind of,"** **"который – which one,"** and **"чей – whose"** that change according to gender, number, and cases

The pronoun **"кто – who"** is used to ask about people and animals.

Кто придёт на вечеринку? – **Who**'ll come to the party?

Все наши друзья придут! – **All our friends** will come!

Кто приходит в офис раньше всех? – **Who** comes to the office earlier than others?

Настя приходит первой. – **Nastya** comes the first.

Pronoun **"что-what"** is used to ask about inanimate objects.

Что ты ищешь? – **What** are you looking for?   Свой **кошелёк**. – My **wallet**.

Pronoun **"сколько-how many/how much"** is used to ask and clarify the quantity of objects or people.

Сколько у тебя отгулов в этом месяце? – **How many** personal days off do you have this month?

У меня пять **отгулов**. – I have five personal **days off**.

Сколько у неё собак? – **How many** dogs does she have?

У неё одна **собака**. – She has one **dog**.

 Pay attention that the forms of these pronouns are the same for singular and plural and will be the same for all genders.

CASE FORMS OF PRONOUNS "КТО", "ЧТО", AND "СКОЛЬКО"

CASE	кто – who	что - what	сколько – how many/how much
NOMINATIVE	кто	что	сколько
GENITIVE	кого	чего	скольких
DATIVE	кому	чему	скольким
ACCUSATIVE	кого	что	сколько
INSTRUMENTAL	кем	чем	сколькими
PREPOSITIONAL	ком	чём	скольких

Pronoun **"какой – what, what kind of"** is used to ask about the attributes of an object or a person.

Какой иностранный язык ты изучаешь? – **What** foreign language do you study?
Какая завтра будет погода? – **What** will the weather be like tomorrow?

Pronoun **"который-which one"** is used to distinguish an object or a person in a row of similar ones.

Который из этих домов ваш? – **Which** of these houses is yours?
Которое платье тебе нравится больше: синее или красное? – **Which** dress do you like more: the blue or the red one?

Pronoun **"чей – whose"** is used to ask about the owner of an object.

Чьи это вещи? – **Whose** stuff is this?
Чьё это пальто? – **Whose** coat is it?

 Pay attention that the forms of these pronouns are different for different genders and numbers and will be different for different cases.

GENDER AND NUMBER OF PRONOUNS "КАКОЙ," "КОТОРЫЙ," AND "ЧЕЙ"

MASCULINE	FEMININE	NEUTRAL	PLURAL
какой	какая	какое	какие
который	которая	которое	которые
чей	чья	чьё	чьи

CASE FORMS OF PRONOUN "КАКОЙ"

CASE	Masculine	Feminine	Neutral	Plural
NOMINATIVE	какой	какая	какое	какие
GENITIVE	какого	какой	какого	каких
DATIVE	какому	какой	какому	каким
ACCUSATIVE	animate = genitive inanimate = nominative	какую	какое	animate = genitive inanimate = nominative
INSTRUMENTAL	каким	какой	каким	какими
PREPOSITIONAL	каком	какой	каком	каких

CASE FORMS OF PRONOUN "КОТОРЫЙ"

CASE	Masculine	Feminine	Neutral	Plural
NOMINATIVE	который	которая	которое	которые
GENITIVE	которого	которой	которого	которых
DATIVE	которому	которой	которому	которым
ACCUSATIVE	animate = genitive inanimate = nominative	которую	которое	animate = genitive inanimate = nominative
INSTRUMENTAL	которым	которой	которым	которыми
PREPOSITIONAL	котором	которой	котором	которых

CASE FORMS OF PRONOUN "ЧЕЙ"

CASE	Masculine	Feminine	Neutral	Plural
NOMINATIVE	чей	чья	чьё	чьи
GENITIVE	чьего	чьей	чьего	чьих
DATIVE	чьему	чьей	чьему	чьим
ACCUSATIVE	animate = genitive inanimate = nominative	чью	чьё	animate = genitive inanimate = nominative
INSTRUMENTAL	чьим	чьей	чьим	чьими
PREPOSITIONAL	чьём	чьей	чьём	чьих

NEGATIVE PRONOUNS

Negative pronouns are used to indicate the fact that an object or a person is absent or doesn't exist. They can be divided into two groups.

1. The ones that start with "ни" and are declined like the corresponding interrogative pronouns.

    никто – nobody   **никакой** – not any kind of
    ничто – nothing   **ничей** – nobody's

    Кто их пригласил? – **Who** has invited them?
    Никто их не приглашал. – **Nobody** invited them.

    Кому они вчера помогли? – **Who** did they help yesterday?
    Они **никому** не помогли. – They didn't help **anyone**.

     Note that, in Russian, double negation is a norm and most often negative pronouns occur with a verb that is negated by means of particle "не." See the examples above.

2. The ones that start with "не" and don't have a nominative form. They are declined like the corresponding interrogative pronouns.

    некого – nobody to   **нечего** – nothing to

    These pronouns are used in impersonal sentences according to the pattern: "Subject in dative + negative pronoun + infinitive verb"

    Мне **нечего** тебе сказать. – I have **nothing to** tell you.
    Тебе **некого** винить. – You have **nobody to** blame.
    Мне **некому** помочь. – I have **nobody to** help me.

     Also pay attention to the cases when these pronouns are used with a preposition. In this case, the "ни" part is separated and the preposition goes between it and the other part.

    Она **ни с кем** не разговаривает. – She doesn't talk **with anyone**.
    Они **ни о чём** не мечтают. – They don't dream **about anything**.
    Мне **не с кем** играть в теннис. – I have **no one** to play tennis **with**.

 **EXERCISES**

1. Match the questions with the images.

(   ) **1.** Чьи это очки?

(   ) **2.** Сколько это стоит?

(   ) **3.** Кто разбил вазу?

(   ) **4.** Которая сумка тяжелее?

(   ) **5.** Какое мороженое твоё любимое?

(   ) **6.** Что лежит в коробке?

A.

D.

B.

E.

C.

F.

100 *Exercises* | *Part IV* | *Chapter II* | *Russian Grammar Made Easy*

2. Match the questions with the answers.

( ) 1. Без какого фрукта ты бы не смог жить? What fruit could you not live without?	A. Она разговаривает о своём новом парне. She's talking about her new boyfriend.
( ) 2. С чем конкретно ты не согласен? With what exactly do you disagree?	B. Я думаю, со сливками. The one with cream I think.
( ) 3. Какой торт мы покупаем: со сливками или с джемом? Which cake do we buy: the one with cream or the one with jam?	C. Не волнуйтесь, это мои дети. Don't worry, these are my kids.
( ) 4. О ком она всё время разговаривает? Who is she talking about all the time?	D. Я бы не смог жить без бананов. I couldn't live without bananas.
( ) 5. Чьи это дети играют одни? Whose kids are playing alone?	E. Мы попросили пять человек. We asked five people.
( ) 6. Скольких людей вы попросили помочь? How many people did you ask to help?	F. Я не согласен с твоими объяснениями. I disagree with your explanations.

3. Choose the correct form of the interrogative pronouns.

1. С _____ ты пойдёшь на выпускной?

   With whom do you go to the prom?

   A. кого   **B.** кем   **C.** кому

2. _____ цветами мы украсим зал?

   With what flowers will we decorate the hall?

   A. какими   **B.** какие   **C.** каких

3. О _____ учениках говорил директор школы?

   About whose students was the school principal talking?

   A. чьими   **B.** чьим   **C.** чьих

4. _____ ты только что звонил?

   Whom have you just called?

   A. кого   **B.** кому   **C.** кто

5. _____ команда прошла в финал?

   What team got to the finals?

   A. какой   **B.** какое   **C.** какая

6. _____ это имя на доске?

   Whose name is on the blackboard?

   A. чьё   **B.** чьи   **C.** чья

7. _____ котёнка мы берём: рыжего или белого?

   Which kitten do we take: the red or the white one?

   A. какому   **B.** какого   **C.** каким

8. _____ ты гордишься больше всего?

   Whom are you proud of most?

   A. кому   **B.** кого   **C.** кем

4. Choose the correct accusative form, paying attention to animate/inanimate nouns.

1. (чей/чьего) рюкзак ты потерял?
   Whose backpack did you lose?

2. (чей/чьего) брата ты обидел?
   Whose brother did you offend?

3. (какой/какого) роман она помнит почти наизусть?
   What novel does she remember almost by heart?

4. Про (который/которого) бизнесмена писали в газете: про бедного или богатого?
   About which businessman did they write in the newspaper: the poor or the rich one?

5. (какие/каких) людей ты не любишь?
   What kind of people do you dislike?

6. (какой/какого) работника ты видишь на этой должности?
   What kind of employee do you see at this post?

5. Use the correct form of the pronoun in brackets.

1. На (что) он приехал в город: на машине или не поезде?   _____
   By what did he come to the town: by car or by train?

2. (какой) мясо ты предпочитаешь?   _____
   What kind of meat do you prefer?

3. (чей) родственником оказался преступник?   _____
   Whose relative did the criminal turn out to be?

4. (кто) сегодня нет в классе?   _____
   Who is absent from the class today?

5. В (какое) обществе ты бы хотел жить?   _____
   In what kind of society would you like to live?

6. О (какой) фильме вы разговариваете?   _____
   About what movie are you talking?

7. (который) ножом ты режешь сыр: большим или маленьким?_____
   With which knife do you cut cheese: with the big or the small one?

8. Напротив (чей) дома находится почта? _____
   Opposite to whose house is the post office situated?

9. (кто) из гостей не нравится чай с сахаром? _____
   Which of the guests doesn't like tea with sugar?

10. (какой) видами спорта ты увлекаешься? _____
    What kinds of sport are you into?

11. (сколько) из своих учеников вы помните по имени? _____
    How many of your pupils do you remember by name?

12. О (который) деле мне вам рассказать: новом или старом? _____
    About which case should I tell you: the new or the old one?

6. Match the questions and the answers.

( ) **1.** Какой ресторан вы выбрали?	**A.** Никто.
( ) **2.** Кто пришёл на концерт?	**B.** Никакой.
( ) **3.** Чей это кот?	**C.** Ничто.
( ) **4.** Что это?	**D.** Ничей.

7. Choose the correct form of the negative pronoun. Remember the way they are used with prepositions.

1. **Этот салат нельзя (ничто/с) сравнить! Он просто волшебный!**
   This salad can't be compared with anything! It's just magical!

   A. нисчем   **B.** ни с чем   **C.** ничего

2. **В этой истории нет (никакой) смысл.**
   This story makes absolutely no sense.

   A. никакому   **B.** никаким   **C.** никакого

3. **Я не советую эту школу (ничей) детям.**
   I don't recommend this school to anybody's children.

   A. ничьим   **B.** ничьего   **C.** ничьему

4. **Не волнуйся (ничто/о)! Всё будет хорошо!**
Don't worry about anything! Everything will be fine!

   A. ни о чём   **B.** ничего   **C.** ниочём

5. **Не рассказывай об этом (никто)!**
Don't tell anyone about it!

   A. никого   **B.** никем   **C.** никому

6. **Мне (нечего) тебя учить. Ты всё знаешь лучше меня!**
I have nothing to teach you. You know everything better than me!

   A. нечему   **B.** нечем   **C.** не о чём

7. **Он (ничто) не интересуется, кроме компьютерных игр.**
He's not interested in anything except computer games.

   A. ничего   **B.** ничему   **C.** ничем

8. **Мне (некого/с) пойти в кино.**
I have no one with whom to go to the cinema.

   A. нескем   **B.** не с кем   **C.** некому

8. Complete the mini-conversations with the proper form of the pronoun in brackets. Check yourself with the audio and role-play the conversations.

I

A: Кого ты позовёшь на день рождения?

B: Я **(никто)** не знаю здесь.   _____

A: Тебе совсем **(некого/с)** проводить время в этом городе!   _____

A: Who will you invite to your birthday?

B: I don't know anyone here.

A: You have absolutely no one with whom to spend time in this town!

II

A: Что она тебе рассказала?

B: (**ничто**) особенного.   _____

A: А я думала, у нас нет (**никакой**) секретов!   _____

B: Я говорю правду! Мы не разговаривали (**ничто/о**) особенном.   _____

A: What did she tell you?

B: Nothing special.

A: And I thought we don't have any kinds of secrets!

B: I'm telling the truth! We didn't talk about anything special!

 III

A: О каком парне ты думаешь?

B: (**никакой/о**)! Я думаю не только о парнях!   _____

A: А мне кажется, твой мозг не занят (**ничто**), кроме свиданий.   _____

A: About what guy are you thinking?

B: None! It's not only guys I think about!

A: And it seems to me your brain is occupied with nothing but dates.

RELATIVE PRONOUNS

Relative pronouns are used to connect parts of complex sentences. They are a connection between the main clause and a subordinate clause. The best part for you as a foreign learner is that the forms and meanings of relative pronouns almost completely coincide with that of interrogative pronouns.

Take a look at all of them in the examples below:

Мы не знаем, **кто** станет нашим новым начальником.
We don't know **who** will become our new boss.

Он сказал, **что** увольняется.
He said **that** he is going to quit.

 Note that the pronoun **"что"** can relate to the whole main part and, in this case, corresponds to the English **"which."**

Она заплакала, **что** очень расстроило меня.
She started crying, **which** made me very upset.

Скажи мне, **сколько** конфет мне купить к празднику?
Tell me **how many** sweets should I buy for the party?

Скажи мне, **какой** цвет тебе больше нравится.
Tell me **what** color you like more.

Жюри не могло решить, **чей** танец был лучше.
The jury could not decide **whose** dance was better.

 The only relative pronoun that is a bit different from its interrogative counterpart is **"который"**. When it's used to connect parts of sentences, it doesn't have the meaning of distinguishing an object in a row of similar objects but has the same meaning as the English **"that/which"**.

Я купила торт, **который** ты посоветовал.

I bought the cake **that** you recommended.

 Note that relative pronouns change according to gender, number, and cases like the corresponding interrogative pronouns.

Это мой одноклассник, с **которым** я поссорился.

This is my classmate with **whom** I quarreled.

It's important to remember that relative pronouns belong to the structure of the subordinate clause and that is why their case form is defined by the "environment" in this clause.

In the example above, "который" substitutes the word "одноклассник". However, it doesn't take its case form, but takes the dative case instead because it's preceded by the preposition "с". Take a look at another example:

Расскажи мне о музыке, **которую** ты слушаешь.

Tell me about the music **that** you listen to.

The pronoun "который" is in feminine singular because it relates to the word "музыка," but it doesn't take the prepositional form because the relative clause has the verb "слушать" that requires the accusative case.

 You can also remember the following pattern that is used quite often:

Demonstrative pronoun in the main clause + the relative pronoun in the subordinate clause.

Это **тот** преступник, **который** ограбил банк.

This is the criminal **that** robbed the bank.

Это **та** женщина, **чей** дом сгорел.

This is **the** woman **whose** house burned down.

INDEFINITE PRONOUNS

Russian indefinite pronouns have a wide range of peculiarities and forms that relate to the shades of meaning and cases of usage. Since this grammar book is aimed to build the basic knowledge, this section will cover the main rules that will allow you to use these pronouns in cases that are most essential for communication and comprehension. Indefinite pronouns are formed with the help of interrogative ones. The pronouns you're going to learn now are divided into two groups:

1. interrogative pronoun + -нибудь

    кто-нибудь – somebody
    что-нибудь – something
    какой-нибудь – some, some kind of
    чей-нибудь – somebody's
    где-нибудь – somewhere
    куда-нибудь – to somewhere
    как-нибудь – somehow

 Indefinite pronouns with this suffix are used to imply a hypothetical object or a person.

Я хочу **что-нибудь** сладкое. – I want **something** sweet.

 Note that the pronoun "какой-нибудь" often corresponds to the concept of an indefinite article in Russian.

Нам нужен **какой-нибудь** новый человек на эту должность.

We need **a** new person for this position.

2. interrogative pronoun + -то

    кто-то – somebody
    что-то – something
    какой-то – some, some kind of
    чей-то – somebody's
    где-то – somewhere
    куда-то – to somewhere
    как-то – somehow

Indefinite pronouns with this suffix are used to imply an object or a person the existence of which the speaker is sure, just doesn't know exactly what its properties are or who/what it is.

Кто-то стучит в дверь.
Someone is knocking on the door.

(I know there is someone because I hear a knock, but I don't know who it is exactly).

У неё **как-то** получилось победить.
She managed to win **somehow**.

(I know she won, but I don't know how she did it).

Indefinite pronouns with **"где", "куда",** and **"как"** don't change grammatically, while the ones with **"кто", "что",** and **"какой"** change like the corresponding interrogative pronouns with **"нибудь"** and **"то"** remaining the same.

 **EXERCISES**

1. Match subordinate clauses with related main clauses and finish the sentences under the images.

( ) 1. Это моя коллега,	**A.** про который я тебе рассказывал.
( ) 2. Он поскользнулся и упал,	**B.** в котором я жил в детстве.
( ) 3. Это тот фильм,	**C.** сколько стоят помидоры.
( ) 4. Мы слышали,	**D.** чья дочь стала врачом.
( ) 5. Это дом,	**E.** что очень рассмешило нас.
( ) 6. Я не помню,	**F.** какую машину купите?
( ) 7. Скажите, пожалуйста,	**G.** что он женится.
( ) 8. Вы решили,	**H.** кто подарил мне эти часы.

2. Use combinations of prepositions and relative pronouns from the box to complete the sentences.

> с которой, на чьи, для кого, после которого,
> на которой, на каком, вместо которых, о чём

1. **Это гора, _____ построили замок.**
   This is a mountain on which a castle was built.

2. **Это работники, _____ они наняли моих знакомых.**
   These are employees, instead of whom they hired my acquaintances.

3. **Это команда, _____я играю в баскетбол по выходным.**
   This is the team with which I play basketball on the weekends.

4. **Это женщина, _____очки я случайно села.**
   This is a woman whose glasses on which I accidentally sat down.

5. Ты знаешь, _____ этаже они живут?

   Do you know on what floor they live?

6. Ого! Ты знаешь, _____ все эти подарки?

   Wow! Do you know for whom all these presents are?

7. Я не слышу, _____ они разговаривают.

   I can't hear about what they're talking.

8. Её выздоровление – это чудо, _____ она стала счастлива!

   Her recovery is a miracle after which she became happy!

3. Choose the correct form of the relative pronoun.

1. Я не понимаю, на _____ языке они разговаривают.

   I don't understand in what language they are talking.

   A. какого   **B.** каком   **C.** каким

2. Это то образование, _____ я мечтаю получить.

   This is the education that I dream to get.

   A. которое   **B.** который   **C.** которому

3. Это студент, _____ имени я не помню.

   This is the student whose name I don't remember.

   A. чьему   **B.** чьего   **C.** чьё

4. Скажите, пожалуйста, _____ специалисту мне лучше позвонить.

   Could you tell me what specialist I'd better call?

   A. какой   **B.** какого   **C.** какому

5. Вы знаете, _____ нужно помочь?

   Do you know who needs to be helped?

   A. кого   **B.** кому   **C.** кем

6. Посоветуй мне, _____ украсить комнату.

   Recommend me with what I should decorate the room.

   A. чем   **B.** чему   **C.** чего

7. Это ваза, в _____ я поставила цветы.

This is the vase in which I placed the flowers.

   A. которой   **B.** которая   **C.** которую

8. Уважаемые пассажиры, _____ вещи потерялись, пожалуйста, подойдите к администратору.

Dear passengers whose belongings were lost, please come to the administrator.

   A. чья   **B.** чьи   **C.** чьё

4. Match the nouns with the corresponding indefinite pronouns.

( ) **1.** камень – stone	**A.** где-то
( ) **2.** в городе – in the city	**B.** кто-то
( ) **3.** в город – to the city	**C.** как-то
( ) **4.** актриса – actress	**D.** что-то
( ) **5.** с помощью – with some help	**E.** какой-то
( ) **6.** странный – strange	**F.** куда-то

5. Choose the correct indefinite pronoun.

1. **Гриша сейчас не дома. Он (где-то/куда-то) в Африке.**

   Grisha is not home now. He's somewhere in Africa.

2. **У тебя на лице (что-то/кто-то) серое.**

   You've got something gray on your face.

3. **Я хочу поехать (где-то/куда-то) далеко.**

   I want to go somewhere far away.

4. **К Вам приходил (какой-то/кто-то) незнакомый человек.**

   An unfamiliar man has come to see you.

5. **Мне (кто-нибудь/что-нибудь) звонил?**

   Has anybody called me?

6. **Он разговаривал (как-то/какой-то) грустно.**

   He was speaking somehow sad.

6. Choose between the indefinite pronouns with -то and -нибудь.

1. (кто-то/кто-нибудь) знает, как доехать до метро?
   Does anybody know how to get to the underground?

2. (кто-то/кто-нибудь) оставил Вам записку.
   Somebody left a note for you.

3. Сергей Иванович ушёл (куда-то/куда-нибудь), но он скоро вернётся.
   Sergey Ivanovich left somewhere but he's going to be back soon.

4. Посмотри! Я нашла (что-то/что-нибудь) необычное!
   Look! I've found something unusual!

5. Мы хотели пойти (куда-то/куда-нибудь) в центре города.
   We wanted to go somewhere in the center of the city.

6. Мне нужен (какой-то/какой-нибудь) интересный фильм на вечер.
   I need an interesting movie for the night.

7. Маша заказала на ужин (что-то/что-нибудь) очень острое.
   Masha has ordered something very spicy for dinner.

8. Они смотрят (какой-то/какой-нибудь) страшный фильм.
   They're watching some scary movie.

7. Choose the correct grammatical form of the indefinite pronoun.

1. Ты знаешь _____ на этом собрании?
   Do you know anyone at this meeting?

   A. кому-нибудь   **B.** кого-нибудь   **C.** ком-нибудь

2. Мы можем поговорить о _____ более серьёзном?
   Can we talk about something more serious?

   A. чём-нибудь   **B.** чему-нибудь   **C.** чего-нибудь

3. Тебе нужно рассказать об этом _____ опытному специалисту.
   You need to tell an experienced specialist about it.

   A. какой-то   **B.** какого-то   **C.** какому-то

4.   В общежитии он живёт с _____ из нашего города.
     In the dormitory, he lives with someone from our town.

     A. кому-то   **B.** кого-то   **C.** кем-то

5.   Смотри! Птицы летают над _____ странным.
     Look! The birds are flying above something weird.

     A. чем-то   **B.** чему-то   **C.** чего-то

6.   Я хочу съесть _____ фрукт на десерт.
     I want to eat some fruit for dessert.

     A. какой-нибудь   **B.** какого-нибудь   **C.** какому-нибудь

7.   В темноте они подошли к _____ твёрдому и холодному.
     In the darkness, they came up to something firm and cold.

     A. чего-то   **B.** чему-то   **C.** что-то

8.   Расскажи мне о _____ из нашего класса!
     Tell me about someone from our class!

     A. ком-нибудь   **B.** кому-нибудь   **C.** кого-нибудь

8. Listen to the conversations and fill in the gaps. Then check, listen again, and role-play. If you want to challenge yourself, try filling in independently.

CONVERSATION 1

A: Здравствуйте! Скажите, пожалуйста, **1)** _____ стоит этот планшет.

B: Здравствуйте! Тридцать тысяч рублей.

A: Ого! Это **2)** _____ дорого!

B: Я понимаю. Я могу показать Вам **3)** _____ более дешёвый вариант.

A: Да, пожалуйста. Я не думаю, **4)** _____ жена поймёт меня, если я куплю сыну такой дорогой планшет.

B: Конечно! Вон тот планшет, **5)** _____ слева от дорогого, стоит всего десять тысяч.

A: Замечательно! Вы можете рассказать **6)** _____ о нём? Он надежный, быстрый, крепкий?

B: Он надёжный и крепкий, но не очень быстрый. Я могу показать Вам

7) _____ чуть более дорогое.

A: Что ж, давайте посмотрим.

A: Hello! Could you tell me how much this tablet costs?

B: Hello! Thirty thousand rubles.

A: Wow! It's somewhat expensive.

B: I understand. I can show you a cheaper option.

A: Do, please. I don't think that my wife will understand me if I buy our son such an expensive tablet.

B: Sure! The tablet that is to the left of the expensive one costs only ten thousand.

A: Great! Can you tell me something about it? Is it reliable, fast, and durable?

B: It's reliable and durable, but it's not very fast. I can show you something a bit more expensive.

A: Well, let's take a look.

🎧 CONVERSATION 2

A: Смотри! **1)** _____ ползёт у тебя по волосам!

B: Где?!

A: Уже не вижу. Этот жук **2)** _____ пропал.

B: Надеюсь, это не тот жук, **3)** _____ укусил меня на прошлой прогулке.

A: Тот жук не укусил тебя! Тебе нужно **4)** _____ делать со своим страхом насекомых!

B: А ты боишься высоты! Мне кажется, **5)** _____ твой страх глупый.

A: Давай не будем сравнивать, **6)** _____ страх больше.

B: О нет! Этот жук **7)** _____ под моей одеждой! Я чувствую его! Помоги мне!

A: Глупышка, это просто **8)** _____ сухой лист.

A: Look! Something is crawling on your hair!

B: Where?!

A: I don't see it now. This beetle disappeared somewhere.

B: Hope it's not the beetle that stung me during our last walk.

A: That beetle didn't sting you! You need to do something about your fear of insects!

B: And you're afraid of heights! It seems to me that your fear is silly.

A: Let's not compare whose fear is bigger.

B: Oh, no! The beetle is somewhere under my clothes! I can feel it! Help me!

A: Silly you, it's just some dry leaf.

MISCELLANEOUS PRACTICE – PRONOUNS

1. Match the personal pronoun with one of its forms and a corresponding possessive pronoun.

( ) **1.** я	**A.** наш	**a.** вам
( ) **2.** ты	**B.** его	**b.** тебе
( ) **3.** мы	**C.** мой	**c.** ему
( ) **4.** вы	**D.** её	**d.** нас
( ) **5.** он	**E.** твой	**e.** них
( ) **6.** она	**F.** их	**f.** ей
( ) **7.** они	**G.** ваш	**g.** мной

2. Choose the correct pronoun.

1. Они всё время ссорятся (друг с другом/ни с кем).

   They constantly quarrel with each other.

2. Перестань вести (себя/сам) так безответственно!

   Stop behaving in such an irresponsible way!

3. Ты уверен, что этот дом (чей-то/ничей)?

   Are you sure this house isn't anybody's?

4. Мне так нравится (тебя/твоя) новая причёска!

   I like your new hair style so much!

5. Скажи мне, (что/что-то) ты имеешь ввиду.

   Tell me what you mean.

6. Ему (ничто/нечего) тебе рассказывать. Ты всё уже знаешь.

   He doesn't have anything to tell you. You know everything already.

7. Вика показала нам (свой/её) новый дом. Она купила его (себе/сама).

   Vika showed us her new house. She bought it by herself.

8. Дайте мне вон (эту/ту) книгу, которая стоит внизу.

   Give me that book over there, the one that's at the bottom.

9. (Тобой/Тебе) нужно больше отдыхать!

   You need to have more rest!

10. Только представь (свой/себе), (сколько/как) денег мы заработаем!

    Just imagine how much money we'll earn!

3. Choose the correct grammatical form of the pronoun.

1. Скажите _____ девушке, что она уронила ключи.
   Tell that girl that she has dropped her keys.

   A. тому   **B.** той   **C.** та

2. Мне _____ рассказать этот секрет.
   I have nobody to tell this secret.

   A. некого   **B.** некем   **C.** некому

3. Я живу в доме, напротив _____ находится музей.
   I live in the house opposite which the museum is situated.

   A. которого   **B.** который   **C.** которому

4. Она закончила университет и может гордиться _____.
   She graduated from the university and can be proud of herself.

   A. собой   **B.** себе   **C.** себя

5. Это статья о _____ знаменитом учёном.
   This is an article about some famous scientist.

   A. какого-то   **B.** какому-то   **C.** каком-то

6. Я не уверена, _____ она оставила это письмо.
   I'm not sure for whom she left this letter.

   A. кого   **B.** кому   **C.** кто

7. Покажи мне, _____ ботинки тебе понравились в этом магазине.
   Show me what shoes you liked in this shop.

   A. каким   **B.** каких   **C.** какие

8. Тебе понравилось то кольцо, _____ я тебе подарила?
   Did you like that ring that I gave you as a present?

   A. которое   **B.** которому   **C.** которого

4. Use the correct form of the pronouns in brackets.

1. Сегодня (я) плохо. Я позвоню (своя) коллеге и попрошу (она) предупредить начальника.

   I feel unwell today. I'll call my colleague and ask her to warn the boss.

2. Можно я подержу (твой) попугая? Как (он) зовут?

   May I hold your parrot? What's his name?

3. Почему я (ничто) не знал об этом?

   Why didn't I know anything about it?

4. (Кто) ты пожелала удачи? Я не услышала.

   Whom did you wish good luck? I didn't hear.

5. Я не знаю, что купить брату на день рождения. У (он) есть всё!

   I don't know what to buy my brother for his birthday. He has everything!

6. Посмотри! Наша бабушка кормит во дворе (чьи-то) кошек.

   Look! Our grandmother is feeding someone's cats in the yard.

7. (Наш) детям так нравится рисовать! Давай наймём (они) учителя!

   Our kids like drawing so much! Let's hire a teacher for them!

8. Кто здесь? Я (никто) не вижу.

   Who is here? I don't see anyone.

5. Listen to the conversation and fill in the pronouns. Then check, listen again, and role-play. If you want to challenge yourself, try filling in independently.

A: Доктор, у **1)** _____ есть вопрос про лекарство, **2)** _____ Вы мне прописали.

B: Пожалуйста. **3)** _____ вопрос?

A: Мне кажется, **4)** _____ не так с дозой. **5)** _____ мне не помогает.

B: 6) _____ таблеток Вы принимаете в день?

A: Три таблетки, как **7)** _____ сказали.

B: Это **8)** _____ ошибка. Я сказал Вам, **9)** _____ нужно принимать пять таблеток.

A: Ой, извините. Наверное, я думала о **10)** _____ другом, когда Вы говорили.

A: Doctor, I have a question about the medicine that you have prescribed me.

B: Welcome. What is the question?

A: It seems to me something is wrong with the dosage. It doesn't help me.

B: How many tablets do you take per day?

A: Three tablets, as you said.

B: This is some mistake. I told you that you need to take five tablets.

A: Oh, I'm sorry. I must have been thinking about something else when you were talking.

CHAPTER

ADJECTIVES

3

PART I
DECLENSION OF ADJECTIVES

Adjectives in Russian agree in gender, number, and case with the nouns they describe. Just like in English, adjectives can precede the noun or follow it.

Красивый цветок. – A **beautiful** flower.
Этот цветок **красивый**. – This flower is **beautiful**.

Different types of adjectives take different endings when declined. Regarding this principle, adjectives are arranged into the following groups, based on the initial form (nominative, masculine, singular):

1. **ending in "ый", "ой", "ий" (but not "ний")**
   новый – new

2. **ending in "ний"**
   синий – deep blue

3. **with stem ending in "ж", "ч", "щ", and unstressed "ш"**
   хороший – good

4. **with stem ending in "г", "к", "х", and stressed "ш"**
   горький – bitter
   большой – big

DECLENSION OF ADJECTIVES ENDING IN "ЫЙ", "ОЙ", "ИЙ"

	Masculine	Feminine	Neutral	Plural
NOMINATIVE	нов**ый**	нов**ая**	нов**ое**	нов**ые**
GENITIVE	нов**ого**	нов**ой**	нов**ого**	нов**ых**
DATIVE	нов**ому**	нов**ой**	нов**ому**	нов**ым**
ACCUSATIVE	animate = genitive inanimate = nominative	нов**ую**	нов**ое**	animate = genitive inanimate = nominative
INSTRUMENTAL	нов**ым**	нов**ой**	нов**ым**	нов**ыми**
PREPOSITIONAL	нов**ом**	нов**ой**	нов**ом**	нов**ых**

DECLENSION OF ADJECTIVES ENDING IN "НИЙ"

	Masculine	Feminine	Neutral	Plural
NOMINATIVE	син**ий**	син**яя**	син**ее**	син**ие**
GENITIVE	син**его**	син**ей**	син**его**	син**их**
DATIVE	син**ему**	син**ей**	син**ему**	син**им**
ACCUSATIVE	animate = genitive inanimate = nominative	син**юю**	син**ее**	animate = genitive inanimate = nominative
INSTRUMENTAL	син**им**	син**ей**	син**им**	син**ими**
PREPOSITIONAL	син**ем**	син**ей**	син**ем**	син**их**

 Adjectives from group three with stem ending in **"ж," "ч," "щ,"** and stressed **"ш"** follow special spelling rules and have **"и"** and **"е"** in their ending instead of **"ы"** and **"о"**.

с новым – с хорошим
with new – with good

о новом – о хорошем
about new – about good

DECLENSION OF ADJECTIVES ENDING IN "Г", "К", "Х", AND STRESSED "Ш"

	Masculine	Feminine	Neutral	Plural
NOMINATIVE	горьк**ий**	горьк**ая**	горьк**ое**	горьк**ие**
GENITIVE	горьк**ого**	горьк**ой**	горьк**ого**	горьк**их**
DATIVE	горьк**ому**	горьк**ой**	горьк**ому**	горьк**им**
ACCUSATIVE	animate = genitive inanimate = nominative	горьк**ую**	горьк**ое**	animate = genitive inanimate = nominative
INSTRUMENTAL	горьк**им**	горьк**ой**	горьк**им**	горьк**ими**
PREPOSITIONAL	горьк**ом**	горьк**ой**	горьк**ом**	горьк**их**

SHORT FORM OF ADJECTIVES

In Russian, adjectives can have a short form.

Она красив**ая**. – Она красив**а**. – She's beautiful.

Although this phenomenon doesn't exist in English, Russian short adjectives and their corresponding English counterparts have the same usage pattern – as part of a predicative construction, i.e., to make a statement about an object or a person. When such situations occur in English, adjectives are usually preceded by the verb **"to be"**.

As you know, Russian verb **"to be" – "быть"** is not used in the present tense, so in present it's just the "noun + adjective" pattern.

Он **голоден**. – He **is hungry**.
Она **была зла**. – She **was angry**.

Short adjectives are mostly used in formal/literature speech, while full forms are more common in everyday speech. However, this division is not strict and you can use short form in a colloquial talk.

 Note that not all adjectives have a short form. For example, "большой – big", "синий – blue". In the exercises below, you'll have a chance to practice some most common short adjectives without going into much complicated detail.

Short adjectives don't change according to cases and coincide with nouns only in gender and number.

DECLENSION OF SHORT ADJECTIVES

MASCULINE	FEMININE	NEUTRAL	PLURAL
bare stem	"-а"	"-о"	"-ы" or "-и"
красив_	красив**а**	красив**о**	красив**ы**

1. The images below are pairs of antonyms with the words written at the bottom. Match the images with their English translations.

(   ) **1.** new – old   (   ) **5.** long – short   (   ) **9.** rich – poor

(   ) **2.** young – old   (   ) **6.** heavy – light   (   ) **10.** fun – boring

(   ) **3.** big – small   (   ) **7.** clean – dirty

(   ) **4.** tall – short   (   ) **8.** full – empty

A.

длинный – короткий

F.

большой – маленький

B.

новый – старый

G.

молодой – старый

C.

полный – пустой

H.

высокий – низкий

D.

весёлый – скучный

I.

чистый – грязный

E.

тяжёлый – лёгкий

J.

богатый – бедный

2. Match the sentences that feature one and the same adjective but in different number/gender forms.

( ) 1. Это лучшее решение.	**A.** Это озеро не глубокое.
( ) 2. Раннее утро – моё любимое время.	**B.** Осторожно! Салат острый.
( ) 3. Острая еда – это не для меня.	**C.** Неужели ты последний?
( ) 4. Ого! Колодец такой глубокий!	**D.** Аня моя бывшая жена.
( ) 5. Мне нравится эта треугольная крыша.	**E.** Я занят в рабочее время.
( ) 6. Обещаю, эта конфета последняя.	**F.** Это лучшая книга.
( ) 7. Он бывший президент.	**G.** Какие милые треугольные печенья!
( ) 8. Сегодня рабочий день.	**H.** Это был ранний вечер.

3. Group the adjectives into the columns based on their gender and number endings.

опасная – dangerous, интересные – interesting, зелёного – green, знаменитое – famous, сложный – difficult, лучшей – best, обычное – ordinary, модные – fashionable, сладкий – sweet, холодных – cold, медленное – slow, мягкий – soft, круглые – round, светлую – light, счастливое – happy, добрый – kind, толстый – fat, слабой – weak, тёмное – dark, здоровая – healthy, красный – red, молодым – young

Masculine	Feminine	Neutral	Plural

4. Choose the right number and gender form of the adjective.

1. Я ненавижу (тёплый/**тёплое**) молоко.
   I hate warm milk.

2. Посмотри! Эта лошадь такая (**быстрая**/быстрые).
   Look! This horse is so fast.

3. У меня две (важное/**важные**) встречи сегодня.
   I've got two important meetings today.

4. Осторожно! Эта собака (злой/**злая**).
   Beware! This dog is angry.

5. Это зеркало (грязный/**грязное**).
   This mirror is dirty.

6. Этот кофе слишком (горькое/**горький**) для меня.
   This coffee is too bitter for me.

7. Мне не нравятся эти (**квадратные**/квадратное) окна.
   I don't like these square windows.

8. Почему эта корова такая (худой/**худая**)?
   Why is this cow so skinny?

9. У неё такое (счастливые/**счастливое**) лицо!
   Her face is so happy!

10. Познакомьтесь, это моя (**младшая**/младшее) сестра.
    Meet my younger sister.

11. Летом даже ночи (жаркая/**жаркие**).
    In summer, even nights are hot.

12. Это очень (**серьёзное**/серьёзный) дело.
    It's a very serious case.

5. Choose the correct case form of the adjective.

1. **Она перешла дорогу с _____ ведром. Это плохая примета.**
   She crossed the road with an empty bucket. It's a bad sign.

   A. пустое   **B.** пустым   **C.** пустому

2. **Кто живёт в этом _____ доме?**
   Who lives in this old house?

   A. старом   **B.** старого   **C.** старый

3. **Я совсем забыла эту _____ песню!**
   I absolutely forgot this fun song!

   A. весёлой   **B.** весёлую   **C.** весёлая

4. **У нас много _____ вещей.**
   We have a lot of old things.

   A. старым   **B.** старые   **C.** старых

5. **Ты пахнешь _____ ароматом.**
   You smell of a sweet aroma.

   A. сладкого   **B.** сладкому   **C.** сладким

6. **Он приехал домой на _____ машине.**
   He came home by a new car.

   A. новой   **B.** новую   **C.** нового

7. **Купи бутылку _____ воды.**
   Buy a bottle of cold water.

   A. холодную   **B.** холодной   **C.** холодная

8. **У меня пять _____ собак!**
   I have five great dogs!

   A. замечательным   **B.** замечательных   **C.** замечательный

6. Use the correct form of the adjective in brackets.

1. Это подарок от моего (старый) друга.   _____
   It's a present from my old friend.

2. Этой (маленький) девочке грустно.   _____
   This little girl is sad.

3. Она порезалась (острый) ножом.   _____
   She cut herself with a sharp knife.

4. Степан нашёл место в (хороший) компании.   _____
   Stepan found a place with a good company.

5. Мы смотрим на город с (высокий) башни.   _____
   We're looking at the town from a tall tower.

6. Всю (следующий) неделю меня не будет в городе.   _____
   I will be out of town all next week.

7. Мне скучно без моего (лучший) друга.   _____
   I'm bored without my best friend.

8. Я в восторге от её (мягкий) голоса.   _____
   I'm excited about her soft voice.

7. Create short forms of the adjectives in brackets.

1. Он (молодой) и (красивый).   _____
   He's young and handsome.

2. Девочка (голодная). Дайте ей поесть.   _____
   The girl is hungry. Give her something to eat.

3. Ночь (короткая).   _____
   The night is short.

4. Мы (счастливые) вместе.   _____
   We're happy together.

5. Это молоко (испорченный).   _____
   This milk is spoiled.

6. Ситуация страшная, а он (спокойный).   _____
   The situation is scary and he's calm.

8. Complete the conversations by creating the right forms of nouns and adjectives. Then check, listen, and role-play.

CONVERSATION I

A: Давай выберем фильм на вечер.

B: Отличная идея! У меня есть много **1) (интересные фильмы)** в списке.

_____

A: Только давай обойдёмся без **2) (романтические комедии)**!

_____

B: Но почему?

A: Потому что я не фанат таких фильмов. Я интересуюсь **3) (научные фильмы)**.

_____

B: О, я знаю, что ты увлекаешься **4) (скучные вещи)**! _____

A: Они не скучные! Они интересные!

B: А как насчёт фильма про приключения?

A: Отличный вариант! Будем смотреть по телевизору или по **5) (новый ноутбук)**?

_____

B: Лучше по телевизору. Мне нравится смотреть фильмы на **6) (большой экран)**.

_____

A: Let's choose a movie for the night.

B: Great idea! I've got lots of interesting movies on the list.

A: But let's do without romantic comedies!

B: But why?

A: Because I'm not a fan of such movies. I'm interested in scientific movies.

B: Oh, I know that you're interested in boring things!

A: They're not boring! They're interesting!

B: And what about an adventure movie?

A: Great option! Will we watch it on TV or on the new laptop?

B: Better on TV. I like watching movies on a big screen.

 CONVERSATION II

A: Где продукты, которые ты купила на рынке?

B: Они в **1) (красная сумка)**. _____

A: А где сумка?

B: Сумка на **2) (квадратный стол)** в кухне. _____

A: Здесь нет **3) (красная сумка)**. _____

B: Не может быть! Посмотри ещё раз.

A: О, теперь я вижу. Она стоит за **4) (синий пакет)** с **5) (детские вещи)**.

_____

B: Да, я купила детям несколько **6) (новые футболки)**. _____

A: А что ты собираешься делать с **7) (жёлтые яблоки)**? _____

B: Я нашла рецепт **8) (яблочный пирог)**! Хочу попробовать. _____

A: Where are the groceries that you've bought at the market?

B: They're in the red bag.

A: And where is the bag?

B: The bag is on the square table in the kitchen.

A: There is no red bag here.

B: It can't be! Look again.

A: Oh, I see now. It is behind the blue plastic bag with kids' clothes.

B: Yes, I bought the kids a few new T-shirts.

A: And what are you going to do with the yellow apples?

B: I found an apple pie recipe! I want to try it.

9. Complete the texts with word combinations using them in the right places and in the right forms.

TEXT I

> милое кафе новый район маленькая машина
> городской автобус большая машина зелёный парк хорошее место

Я живу в **1)** _____. Это **2)** _____,
но здесь пока что мало магазинов. Мой дом далеко от центра города, но здесь много

3) _____ и **4)** _____. Я езжу на

работу на **5)** _____. У меня пока что нет своей машины.

Я хочу купить **6)** _____, потому что я живу одна и мне не

нужна **7)** _____.

I live in a new district. It's a good place, but there are not many shops here yet. My house is far away from the city center, but there are many green parks and nice cafes here. I go to work by the city bus. I don't have a car of my own yet. I want to buy a small car because I live alone and I don't need a big car.

TEXT II

> новый рецепт солёный суп готовая еда острый перец
> честный человек хороший муж

Моя жена не умеет готовить. Вчера она приготовила слишком **1)** _____

_____, а в рагу было очень много **2)** _____. Я хочу

быть **3)** _____, но ещё я хочу быть **4)** _____

_____. Я не могу врать своей жене и говорить, что её еда вкусная. Сегодня

она готовит по **5)** _____. Надеюсь, всё будет хорошо, и мы не

будем заказывать **6)** _____, как в прошлый раз.

My wife can't cook. Yesterday she cooked a soup that was too salty and there was too much spicy pepper in the stew. I want to be a good husband, but I want to be an honest man, too. I can't lie to my wife and say that her food is delicious. Today she's cooking according to a trendy recipe. I hope everything will be fine and we won't have to order ready-made food like last time.

PART II
DEGREES OF COMPARISON OF ADJECTIVES

Degrees of comparison of adjectives in the Russian language follow a logic that is quite similar to that of building English comparative forms. There are three degrees of comparison:

1. **Positive. Simply denotes a quality of the noun.**

   Это большое яблоко. – It's a big apple.

2. **Comparative. Compares the qualities of nouns to each other.**

   Моё яблоко больше, чем твоё. – My apple is bigger than yours.

3. **Superlative. States that the quality is superior to that of other objects.**

   Это яблоко самое большое. – This apple is the biggest.

| большой | больше | самый большой |

 Remember that not all adjectives can have comparative forms. For example, they include adjectives that denote shapes and colors.

COMPARATIVE DEGREE

Just like in English, there are two options for creating the comparative degree – a simple and a compound one.

How to create a simple comparative degree of an adjective

1. Take an adjective in its nominative singular form.
2. Remove the gender ending.
3. Add the ending "-ee".

Это платье красивое, но моё **красивее**. – This dress is beautiful but mine is **more beautiful**.

The good news is that adjectives in their simple comparative degree are not declined according to cases and take the same ending for all genders and numbers.

However, there are a few spelling rules that you should remember.

1. If an adjective stem ends in **"-г", "-к", "-х"** or **"-д", "-т", "-ст"**, then only one "-e" is added.

громкий – громче   loud – louder

2. If the stem ends in **"-г", "-к", "-х"**, the final consonant is replaced by **"-ж", "-ч", "-ш"**, respectively.

тихий – тише   quiet – quieter

3. If the stem ends in **"-ст"**, the cluster is replaced by **"-щ"**.

простой – проще   simple – simpler

IRREGULAR COMPARATIVE FORMS

хороший – лучше – good – better
плохой – хуже – bad – worse
маленький – меньше – small – smaller
близкий – ближе – close – closer
большой – больше – big – bigger
высокий – выше – high – higher
глубокий – глубже – deep – deeper
далёкий – дальше – far – farther
дешёвый – дешевле – cheap – cheaper
долгий – дольше – long – longer

короткий – короче – short – shorter
лёгкий – легче – light – lighter
молодой – моложе – young – younger
поздний – позже – late – later
ранний – раньше – early – earlier
редкий – реже – rare – more rare
сладкий – слаще – sweet – sweeter
старый – старше – old – older
широкий – шире – wide – wider

How to create a compound comparative degree of an adjective

1. Take the adjective as it is;
2. Add the word "**более – more**" if you want to imply superiority;
3. Add the word "**менее – less**" if you want to imply inferiority.

The words "более" and "менее" don't change, no matter what form the noun takes, while the adjectives follow regular declension rules.

Мы купили **более просторный** дом. – We've bought a **more spacious** house.

SUPERLATIVE DEGREE

There are two options for creating the superlative degree – a simple and a compound one. However, the simple form contradicts its name as it's more difficult both in terms of its creation and declension.

Moreover, the simple form of the superlative degree is more characteristic for scientific and formal speech. Taking these aspects into account, we'll start with the compound form to make things easier for you at the start.

How to create a compound superlative degree of an adjective

*   Take the adjective in the nominative case and in the gender the noun requires;
*   Add the words "самый", "самая", "самое", or "самые" for masculine, feminine, neutral, and plural forms, respectively.

Зачем ты купила **самое дорогое** колье? – Why did you buy **the most expensive** necklace?

 Remember that both words have to agree with the noun in gender, number, and case.

Ты будешь отлично выглядеть в **самом дорогом** колье! – You'll look great in **the most expensive** necklace!

How to create a simple superlative degree of an adjective

*   Take the adjective in its initial form;
*   Remove the ending, leaving the stem only;
*   Add "**ейш**";
*   Add ending "**-ий**", "**-ая**", "**-ое**", or "**-ые**" for masculine, feminine, neutral, and plural forms, respectively.

Note that these adjectives are declined like the ones ending in **"-ж"**, **"-ш"**, **"-ч"**, and **"-щ"**.

Премию дали нашему **новейшему** роботу. – The award was given to our **most recent** robot.

 There is also a way to imply that a person or an object possesses a characteristic that is the highest/lowest or best/worst among others in the group. For this purpose, the words **"наиболее" and "наименее"** are used and these words stay the same regardless of any grammatical forms.

Он выбрал **наиболее интересный** вариант. – He chose the **most interesting** option.
Он выбрал **наименее интересный** вариант. – He chose the **least interesting** option.

There is one more way of creating the superlative degree and it's very widespread in everyday conversations. To form it, you need to use the simple comparative form + the words **"всех"** or **"всего"** that mean **"than anyone"** or **"than anything/most of all"**.

Мой внук **умнее всех** в классе. – My grandson is **the smartest** in his class.
Эти пирожные мне понравились **больше всего**. – I liked these cakes **most of all**.

IRREGULAR SIMPLE SUPERLATIVE

плохой – худший – bad – worst
маленький – меньший – small – the smallest
короткий – кратчайший – short – the shortest
хороший – лучший – good – the best

 Note an important difference between Russian and English. While in English the use of a simple or compound form depends on the number of syllables in the adjective, in Russian it depends on what part of the sentence the adjective is.

If the adjective is part of a complex predicate (part of construction "to be + adjective"), then you can use any form you like best. If the adjective precedes a noun and acts as a descriptive attribute, you can only use the compound form.

Compare:

Мой дом **дороже**. – Мой дом **более дорогой**. – My house is **more expensive**.
Мы купили **более дорогой** дом. – We bought a **more expensive** house.

 **EXERCISES**

1. Create their comparative (simple) and superlative forms (compound) of the adjectives below.

1. высокий

   _____

2. молодой

   _____

3. холодный

   _____

4. грязный

   _____

5. сильный

   _____

6. толстый

   _____

2. Match the adjectives with their comparative and superlative forms.

	POSITIVE	COMPARATIVE	SUPERLATIVE
( )	**1.** хороший – good	**A.** более главный	**a.** самый твёрдый
( )	**2.** твёрдый – hard	**B.** глубже	**b.** самый сладкий
( )	**3.** тяжёлый – heavy	**C.** лучше	**c.** главнее всего
( )	**4.** глубокий – deep	**D.** тяжелее	**d.** самый скучный
( )	**5.** быстрый – quick	**E.** более скучный	**e.** самый быстрый
( )	**6.** сладкий – sweet	**F.** твёрже	**f.** лучший
( )	**7.** главный – main	**G.** быстрее	**g.** самый глубокий
( )	**8.** скучный – boring	**H.** слаще	**h.** тяжелее всех

3. Choose between the comparative and superlative form.

1. Это (самый страшный/страшнее) фильм на свете!

   It's the scariest movie in the world!

2. Наш новый диван (самый удобный/более удобный), чем старый.

   Our new sofa is more comfortable than the old one.

3. Она стала (самой уверенной/увереннее) после колледжа.

   She became more confident after college.

4. Он (самый весёлый/более весёлый) клоун во всём цирке!

   He's the funniest clown in the whole circus!

5. Вы выбрали (худший/хуже) вариант из всех.

   You've chosen the worst option of all.

6. Твоё решение (самое простое/проще), чем моё.

   Your decision is easier than mine.

7. Сегодня (самый жаркий/жарче) день в году.

   Today is the hottest day of the year.

8. Моя старая подушка была (самая мягкая/мягче), чем новая.

   My old pillow was softer than the new one.

4. Choose the correct grammatical form of the adjective in the comparative or superlative degree.

1. **На свете нет _____ человека, чем мой брат.**
   There is no more loyal person in the world than my brother.

   A. более верному   **B.** более верного   **C.** более верном

2. **Это книга о _____ месте на планете.**
   This book is about the most dangerous place on the planet.

   A. самом опасном   **B.** самому опасному   **C.** самым опасным

3. **Я еду в лагерь со своим _____ другом.**
   I'm going to a camp with my best friend.

   A. лучшим   **B.** лучшего   **C.** лучший

4. **После переезда мы живём в _____ доме.**
   After moving, we live in a less spacious house.

   A. менее просторному   **B.** менее просторного   **C.** менее просторном

5. **Она вышла замуж за _____ из своих парней.**
   She married the worst of her boyfriends.

   A. худшим   **B.** худшего   **C.** худшему

6. **Два стакана вашей _____ колы, пожалуйста!**
   Two glasses of your coldest cola, please!

   A. самой холодной   **B.** самая холодная   **C.** самую холодную

7. **Они запатентовали свои _____ изобретения.**
   They patented their most recent inventions.

   A. новейшим   **B.** новейшие   **C.** новейших

8. **Дай мне ту _____ сумку.**
   Give me that less heavy bag.

   A. менее тяжёлой   **B.** менее тяжёлая   **C.** менее тяжёлую

5. Complete the sentences by making the right forms of the adjectives in brackets, either comparative or superlative.

1. **Эта дорога (короткий) всех.**
   This road is the shortest of all.

   _____

2. **Не обижай тех, кто (слабый) тебя.**
   Don't offend those who are weaker than you.

   _____

3. **Этот хомячок (милый) на свете!**
   This little hamster is the cutest in the world.

   _____

4. **Сложно быть (младший) в семье.**
   It's hard to be the youngest in the family.

   _____

5. **Моя бабушка (добрый) всех!**
   My grandmother is the kindest of all!

   _____

6. **Тебе нужно быть (серьёзный), если ты хочешь эту работу.**
   You should be more serious if you want this job.

   _____

7. **Завтра мне нужно проснуться (ранний).**
   I need to wake up earlier tomorrow.

   _____

8. **Погода стала (холодный) после дождя.**
   The weather became colder after the rain.

   _____

9. **Это было (сложный) время в моей жизни!**
   That was the most difficult time in my life!

   _____

10. **На рынке овощи стоят (дешёвый).**
    The vegetables are cheaper at the market.

    _____

11. **Твой пирог (вкусный) из всех на фестивале.**
    Your pie is the tastiest of all at the festival.

    _____

12. **Моя мама (старший) папы на два года.**
    My mother is two years older than my father.

    _____

6. Fill in the adjectives from the box to complete the conversations. Check yourself, listen, and role-play.

CONVERSATION I

быстрее лучше лучшие лучшая лучше умнее

A: Мы должны решить, чья собака едет на соревнования.

B: Конечно же моя! Мой Солдат **1)** _____, чем твоя Стрела.

A: Это почему? Моя Стрела **2)** _____ собака в нашем районе!

B: Может быть, но не в городе! Тем более Солдат **3)** _____, чем Стрела.

A: Да, Солдат быстрый пёс, но моя собака **4)** _____, чем твоя.

Она понимает команды **5)** _____ всех!

B: Жаль, что на соревнования может ехать только одна собака.

A: Да, они обе **6)** _____!

A: We have to decide whose dog goes to the competition.

B: Of course, mine! My Soldier is better than your Arrow.

A: Why's that? My Arrow is the best dog in the district!

B: Maybe, but not in the city! Moreover, Soldier is faster than Arrow.

A: Yes, Soldier is a fast dog, but my dog is smarter than yours. It understands instructions better than anyone!

B: It's a pity that only one dog can go to the competition.

A: Yeah, they both are the best!

терпеливее	реже	менее престижный	старше	ближе	лучшее	

A: Я слышала, твой сын поступил в университет. Мои поздравления!

B: Да, спасибо! Но мне немного грустно.

A: Почему?

B: Мы будем **1)** _____ видеться.

A: Понимаю! Но он мог поступить в университет, который **2)** _____ к дому.

B: Да, но тот университет **3)** _____, а я хочу, чтобы мой сын

получил **4)** _____ образование!

A: Тогда тебе нужно быть **5)** _____.

B: Согласна. Просто мой сын стал **6)** _____, и это немного грустно.

A: I've heard your son has entered a university. Congratulations!

B: Yes, thank you! But I'm a bit sad.

A: Why?

B: We will see each other more rarely.

A: I understand! But he could enter a university that is closer to home.

B: Yes, but that university is less prestigious and I want my son to get the best education!

A: Then you should be more patient.

B: I agree. It's just that my son became older and I'm a bit sad.

MISCELLANEOUS PRACTICE – ADJECTIVES

1. Match the prepositions with the combinations of nouns and adjectives that they require.

( ) **1.** через	**A.** свободного времени
( ) **2.** без	**B.** высокими зданиями
( ) **3.** между	**C.** глубокое озеро
( ) **4.** на	**D.** быстром поезде

2. Choose the correct form of the adjective.

1. **В этот раз твои результаты _____, чем в прошлый.**
   This time your results are worse than last time.

   A. хорошие   **B.** хуже   **C.** более плохие

2. **Лорд – _____ собака во дворе.**
   Lord is the angriest dog in the yard.

   A. самая злая   **B.** более злая   **C.** злая

3. **Я заказала две _____ пиццы.**
   I ordered two big pizzas.

   A. наибольшие   **B.** большие   **C.** более большие

4. **В молодости я был _____, но счастливее.**
   In my youth, I was poorer but happier.

   A. беднее   **B.** бедный   **C.** самый бедный

5. **Она занимается _____ спортом.**
   She's doing extreme sports.

   A. самым экстремальным   **B.** более экстремальным   **C.** экстремальным

6. **Это лекарство _____. Я рекомендую его.**
   This medicine is safer. I recommend it.

   A. более безопасное   **B.** безопасное   **C.** самое безопасное

7. **Я не полечу на этом _____ самолёте!**
   I'm not flying in this old plane!

   A. самом старом   **B.** более старом   **C.** старом

8. Это _____ решение из всех!

It's the worst decision of all!

A. хуже   **B.** худшее   **C.** плохое

3. Complete the groups of sentences below with different forms of the same adjective.

A. интересный

1. Это история с _____ концом.

It's a story with an interesting ending.

2. Давай посмотрим какое-нибудь _____ кино.

Let's watch an interesting movie.

3. Наши партнёры предложили _____ варианты.

Our partners suggested interesting options.

4. Она нашла новую _____ работу.

She found a new interesting job.

белый

1. Это варенье _____. Оно со сливками?

This jam is white. Does it have cream in it?

2. Смотри, какая красивая _____ птица!

Look, what a beautiful white bird!

3. Твои _____ кроссовки слишком грязные.

Your white sneakers are too dirty.

4. Аптека находится возле того _____ здания.

The drugstore is situated near that white building.

любимый

1. Я не могу спать без своей _____ подушки.

I can't sleep without my favorite pillow.

2. Как жаль! В меню нет моего _____ салата.

What a pity! My favorite salad is not on the menu.

3. Радость – моё _____ слово.

Joy is my favorite word.

4. Это фильм о моей _____ писательнице.

This is a movie about my favorite female writer.

4. Fill in the gaps by creating the right forms of adjectives in brackets in order to complete the conversation. Role-play after checking yourself

A: Здравствуйте, **1) (дорогой)** _____ радиослушатели! Наш

сегодняшний гость – автор **2) (популярный)** _____ книги о

3) (вкусный) _____ и **4) (здоровый)** _____

еде. Здравствуйте, Татьяна!

B: Здравствуйте, Анатолий! Здравствуйте, мои читатели и слушатели этой передачи!

A: Татьяна, Ваша книга стала бестселлером всего за несколько недель. В чём секрет?

B: Никакого **5) (особенный)** _____ секрета нет. Мне кажется, дело

в том, что рецепты **6) (простой)** _____, а ингредиенты **7) (обычный)**

_____.

A: Возможно! Я видел несколько рецептов и там не было **8) (экзотический)**

_____ продуктов!

B: Да! Это мой девиз – **9) (вкусный)** _____ блюдо – это

10) (несложный) _____ блюдо!

A: Hello, dear radio audience! Our today's guest is the author of a popular book about delicious and healthy food. Hello, Tatiana!

B: Hello, Anatoliy! Hello, dear readers and the audience of this show!

A: Tatiana, your book has become a bestseller in just a few weeks. What's the secret?

B: There is no special secret. It seems to me that it's because the recipes are simple and the ingredients are common.

A: Likely! I've seen a few recipes and there were no exotic foodstuffs!

B: Yeah, it's my motto – a delicious dish is an uncomplicated dish!

CHAPTER

VERBS

4

Russian verbs have the following grammatical categories:

1. aspect – imperfective (do) and perfective (have done)
2. tense – present, past, and future
3. 1st and 2nd conjugation (for the present tense)
4. person and number (for the present and the future tenses)
5. gender and number (for the past tense)
6. mood – indicative (I do), imperative (do, please) and subjunctive (would do, not covered in this book)
7. voice – active and passive (not covered in this book)

PART I
ASPECT OF VERBS

Aspect is a crucial category of the Russian verb that promotes correct comprehension and creation of verb forms in all tenses. Understanding this concept will make it easier for you to master the tenses of the Russian verb.

Aspect denotes whether the action is complete, in progress, or is a frequent one. There are two aspects in Russian:

1. imperfective – несовершенный
2. perfective – совершенный

Almost all Russian verbs have two aspects:

читать – read

прочитать – have read

Imperfective verbs:

1. Can be used in all tenses;
2. Denote repeated or habitual actions;

Present: Я **хожу** в бассейн по вторникам. – I **go** to the swimming pool on Tuesdays.
Past: Раньше я много **читал**. – I used to **read** a lot.
Future: Я **буду вставать** раньше на следующей неделе. – I **will get up** earlier next week.

3. Denote continuous actions or actions in progress;

Present: Настя **моет** пол. – Nastya **is washing** the floor.
Past: Мы **готовили** и **болтали**. – We **were cooking** and **chatting**.
Future: Они **будут путешествовать** весь год. – They **will be travelling** all year.

4. Someone's life experiences (for the past tense);

Я **видел** снежного человека! Правда! – I **saw** a yeti! It's true!

Perfective verbs:

1. Can be used in the past and the future, because perfective verbs emphasize the result and the result can't be achieved in the present,
2. Implies that the action was or will be completed.
3. Implies that it was a one-time action.

Past: Маша **приготовила** обед. – Masha **cooked** dinner.
The emphasis is on the fact that she cooked it completely, the action is finished.
Future: Она **приготовит** обед для гостей. – She **will cook** dinner for the guests.
The emphasis is on the fact that by the time the guests come, the dinner will be ready.

 How to differentiate between imperfective and perfective verbs? First, it depends on your situation. If you see or hear a verb, you can:

1. Check the dictionary. Most of them have a corresponding indication.
2. Be guided by certain prefixes and suffixes.

Common perfective prefixes:

"По-"	"С-"	"На-"
положить – lay down	**с**делать – do	**на**писать – write
почитать – read	**с**петь – sing	**на**рисовать – draw
посмотреть – watch	**с**варить – cook	**на**печатать – type
полюбить – like		

Common imperfective suffixes:

"-ать"	"-ивать"
реш**ать** – decide	спраш**ивать** – ask
рис**овать** – draw	разговар**ивать** – talk
мечт**ать** – dream	заслуж**ивать** – deserve

Some verbs are irregular, like "класть" and "положить" for "lay down." The verbs that end in **"-ать"** and **"-ять"** have **"и"** instead of **"а"** or **"я"** in imperfective verbs.

объясн**ять** – объясн**ить** – explain

If you write or talk, then you need to decide which form you need and know how to create it. This skill takes practice and you'll have a lot, both in this part and in the parts below.

HERE IS A LIST OF SOME OF THE MOST COMMON IMPERFECTIVE/PERFECTIVE PAIRS FOR YOU TO STUDY AND REFER TO.

IMPERFECTIVE	PERFECTIVE	TRANSLATION
думать	подумать	to think
верить	поверить	to believe
работать	поработать	to work
смотреть	посмотреть	to watch
казаться	показаться	to seem
пытаться	попытаться	to try
делать	сделать	to do, to make
видеть	увидеть	to see
мочь	смочь	to be able to
хотеть	захотеть	to want
ждать	подождать	to wait
писать	написать	to write
читать	прочитать	to read
покупать	купить	to buy
готовить	приготовить	to cook
брать	взять	to take
класть	положить	to lay down

садиться	сесть	to sit down
решать	решить	to decide
продолжать	продолжить	to continue
слышать	услышать	to hear
знать	узнать	to know
понимать	понять	to understand
рассказывать	рассказать	to tell
давать	дать	to give
отвечать	ответить	to answer
начинать	начать	to begin
спрашивать	спросить	to ask
помогать	помочь	to help
вспоминать	вспомнить	to remember
отвечать	ответить	to answer

1. Match pairs of imperfective/perfective verbs with the images that illustrate incomplete/completed actions.

(   ) **1.** готовить – приготовить
(   ) **2.** писать – написать
(   ) **3.** лечить – вылечить

(   ) **4.** покупать – купить
(   ) **5.** смотреть – посмотреть
(   ) **6.** отвечать – ответить

A.

B.

C.

D.

E.

F.

2. Match the columns to create pairs of imperfective/perfective verbs. Underline the parts of words that make the difference between the forms. Note that they can be in different tense forms.

IMPERFECTIVE	PERFECTIVE
( ) **1.** рассказывать	**A.** сказала
( ) **2.** начинала	**B.** открыть
( ) **3.** вспомнить	**C.** взял
( ) **4.** говорила	**D.** рассказать
( ) **5.** открывать	**E.** поверишь
( ) **6.** знали	**F.** начала
( ) **7.** берёт	**G.** узнали
( ) **8.** веришь	**H.** вспоминали

3. Match pairs of sentences that have imperfective/perfective verbs with the theoretical part that explains the difference between them.

( ) **1.**	**A.**
A. Сегодня наш начальник **решает**, кого повысить. Today the boss is deciding whom to promote. **B.** Завтра наш начальник **решит**, кого повысить. Tomorrow our boss will decide whom to promote.	The difference between the imperfective and perfective forms is in the prefix **"по-."** In **A**, the verb denotes a habitual, repeated action. In **B**, the verb denotes a completed action.

( ) 2. **A.** По вечерам мы с мужем **смотрим** сериалы. In the evenings, my husband and I watch series. **B.** Вчера мы **посмотрели** крутой сериал! We watched a cool series yesterday.	**B.** The difference between the imperfective and perfective forms is in the roots. In **A**, the verb denotes a habitual action. In **B**, the verb denotes a one-time action.
( ) 3. **A.** Когда я ездила в столицу, я **видела** президента. When I went to the capital, I saw the president. **B.** Женщина **увидела** дым и позвонила в пожарную службу. The woman saw smoke and called the fire brigade.	**C.** The difference between the imperfective and perfective forms is in the suffixes **"-а"/"-и"**. In **A**, the verb denotes an action in progress. In **B**, the verb denotes an action that will be completed in the future.
( ) 4. **A.** Нельзя **брать** чужие вещи без спроса! One can't take someone else's things without asking! **B.** Не забудь **взять** в поход тёплые вещи! Don't forget to take warm clothes when you go hiking.	**D.** The difference between the imperfective and perfective forms is in the prefix "-у". In **A**, the verb denotes personal experience. In **B**, the verb denotes a one-time, completed action.

4. Below are pairs of sentences with imperfective/perfective verbs. Mark the verbs accordingly.

A. **1. Какой аромат! Мама готовит торт.**

What an aroma! Mom is cooking a cake.

2. Посмотри, какой замечательный торт приготовила мама.

Look what a great cake Mom has cooked.

_____

B. **1. Я придумала отличное решение!**

I thought of an excellent solution!

2. Я всегда думаю о тебе.

I always think of you.

_____

C. **1. Жаль, что Жанна не сможет прийти.**

It's a pity Jeanne won't be able to come.

2. Жанна ходит в спортзал по субботам.

Jeanne goes to the gym on Saturdays.

_____

D. **1. Завтра я напишу тебе письмо.**

I'll write you a letter tomorrow.

2. Она будет писать эту книгу два года.

She'll be writing this book for two years.

_____

E. **1. Пока я мыла посуду, моя сестра смотрела телевизор.**

While I was washing the dishes, my sister was watching TV.

2. Я помыла посуду и включила телевизор.

I washed the dishes and turned on the TV.

_____

5. Choose between the imperfective and perfective form of the verb in brackets, depending on the meaning of the sentence.

1. Я всегда (покупаю/купила) одежду онлайн.
   I always buy clothes online.

2. Я (покупаю/купила) новую блузку.
   I bought a new blouse.

3. Что вы будете (делать/сделал) на выходных?
   What will you be doing on the weekend?

4. Она никогда не (хотела/захочет) вернуться сюда.
   She'll never want to come back here.

5. Мне (казалось/показалось), что он расстроен.
   It seemed to me he was upset.

6. Я (буду работать/поработали) на следующих выходных.
   I will be working next weekend.

7. Она всегда (хотела/захочет) стать врачом.
   She always wanted to become a doctor.

8. Она (поверила/верила) мне без объяснений.
   She believed me without any explanations.

9. Макар (делать/сделал) большую ошибку.
   Makar has made a big mistake.

10. В детстве мне (казалось/показалось), что мир лучше.
    Back in my childhood, it seemed to me that the world was a better place.

11. Мы хорошо (буду работать/поработали) и можем отдохнуть!
    We worked well and can have a rest!

12. Она никогда не (поверила/верила) в привидения.
    She has never believed in ghosts.

6. Complete the conversation by choosing the right verb. Role-play after checking.

A: Коля, у тебя есть мечта?

B: Да! Я мечтаю **1)** _____ книгу!

A: Интересно! Ты уже **2)** _____, о чём?

B: Ещё нет. Я **3)** _____.

A: Помнишь, в детстве дедушка **4)** _____ нам много интересных историй. Они могут подойти для книги.

B: Ого! Я никогда не **5)** _____ об этом! Отличная идея!

A: Мы **6)** _____ их с таким интересом!

B: О, да! Я **7)** _____ первую, когда мне было пять и помню её сейчас.

A: Можешь **8)** _____ её мне?

B: Конечно!

1. ( )	A. написать	B. писать	C. пишу
2. ( )	A. думал	B. думаешь	C. придумал
3. ( )	A. придумал	B. думаю	C. придумаю
4. ( )	A. рассказать	B. рассказывал	C. рассказал
5. ( )	A. придумать	B. думал	C. придумывать
6. ( )	A. услышать	B. услышали	C. слушали
7. ( )	A. услышал	B. слушал	C. слушали
8. ( )	A. рассказывать	B. рассказать	C. рассказываю

A: Kolya, do you have a dream?

B: Yes! I dream of writing a book!

A: Interesting! Have you already thought of what it will be about?

B: Not yet. I'm thinking.

A: Do you remember that grandpa used to tell us many interesting stories in our childhood? They can be suitable for a book.

B: Wow! I've never thought of it! Great idea!

A: We used to listen to them with such interest!

B: Oh, yeah! I heard the first one when I was five and I still remember it.

A: Can you tell me?

B: Sure!

PART II
THE PRESENT TENSE

The present tense in Russian expresses both habitual and current actions, and is also used to express universal truths.

For example:

Сейчас я **читаю**. – I **am reading** now (current action)
Обычно я **читаю** вечером. – I usually **read** in the evening (habitual)
Солнце **встаёт** на востоке. – The sun **rises** in the East (universal truth)

So, Russian present tense corresponds to several English present tenses – present simple, present continuous, and present perfect continuous.

All verbs in the present tense, except the verb "быть – to be", change according to the person and number, which is expressed in the ending.

> The verb "быть – to be" is not used in the present tense, it's just omitted.

Compare:

Сегодня я слишком занят. – I am too busy today.
Моя мама переводчица. – My mother is a translator.

In order to create a present tense form, you should first decide in which of the two conjugation groups the verb belongs to, and then choose the corresponding ending.

VERBS CONJUGATION IN THE PRESENT TENSE

1ST CONJUGATION VERBS

1. All the verbs that end in **"-ать"**, except these four: **гнать (chase)**, **держать (hold)**, **слышать (hear)**, **дышать (breathe)** that belong to the 2nd conjugation.

   Игр**ать** (play) – Я игра**ю** (I play) – 1st conjugation
   Слышать (hear) – Я слыш**у** (I hear) – 2nd conjugation

2. All the verbs that end in **"-ять"**, **"-уть"**, **"-ють"**, **"-ыть"**, **"-чь"**.

Гул**ять** (walk) – Я гуля**ю** (I walk)
М**ыть** (wash) – Я мо**ю** (I wash)

3. All the verbs that end in **"-еть"**, except for **терпеть (bear, suffer)**, **вертеть (spin)**, **обидеть (offend)**, **ненавидеть (hate)**, **зависеть (depend)**, **смотреть (watch)**, and **видеть (see)**.

Бол**еть** (To be sick) – Я боле**ю** (I am sick)

4. Two verbs that end in **"-ить"**: **брить (shave, transitive)** and **стелить (spread, lay, in the context of a tablecloth or bed linen)**

Бр**ить** (Shave) – Я бре**ю** (I shave)

To form the verb in the present tense, remove "ть" from the infinitive and add the corresponding ending.

PRESENT TENSE ENDINGS FOR THE 1ST CONJUGATION

PRONOUN/PERSON	ENDING	EXAMPLE
я (1st person singular)	**"-ю"**	Я игра**ю**. – I play. Я гуля**ю**. – I walk.
ты (2nd person singular)	**"-ешь"**	Ты игра**ешь**. – You play. Ты гуля**ешь**. – You walk.
он, она (3rd person singular)	**"-ет"**	Она игра**ет**. – She plays. Он гуля**ет**. – He walks.
мы (1st person plural)	**"-ем"**	Мы игра**ем**. – We play. Му гуля**ем**. – We walk.
вы (2nd person plural)	**"-ете"**	Вы игра**ете**. – You play. Вы гуля**ете**. – You walk.
они (3rd person plural)	**"-ют"**	Они игра**ют**. – They play. Они гуля**ют**. – They walk.

2ᴺᴰ CONJUGATION VERBS

1. All verbs that end in **"-ить"**, except **брить (shave)** and **стелить (spread, lay).**

Говор**ить** (talk) – Я говор**ю** (I talk)

2. The seven **"-еть"** verbs: **bear, suffer (терпеть), вертеть (spin), обидеть (offend), ненавидеть (hate), зависеть (depend), смотреть (watch), and видеть (see).**

Смотр**еть** (watch) – Я смотр**ю** (I watch)

3. The four **"-ать"** verbs: **гнать (chase), держать (hold), слышать (hear), дышать (breathe).**

Держ**ать** (hold) – Она держ**ит** (She holds)

To form the verb in the present tense, remove three final letters from the infinitive and add the corresponding ending.

PRESENT TENSE ENDINGS FOR THE 2ᴺᴰ CONJUGATION

PRONOUN/PERSON	ENDING	EXAMPLE
я (1ˢᵗ person singular)	**"-ю"**	Я говор**ю**. – I talk. Я смотр**ю**. – I watch.
ты (2ⁿᵈ person singular)	**"-ишь"**	Ты говор**ишь**. – You talk. Ты смотр**ишь**. – You watch.
он, она (3ʳᵈ person singular)	**"-ит"**	Она говор**ит**. – She talks. Он смотр**ит**. – He watches.
мы (1ˢᵗ person plural)	**"-им"**	Мы говор**им**. – We talk. Му смотр**им**. – We watch.
вы (2ⁿᵈ person plural)	**"-ите"**	Вы говор**ите**. – You talk. Вы смотр**ите**. – You watch.
они (3ʳᵈ person plural)	**"-ят"**	Они говор**ят**. – They talk. Они смотр**ят**. – They watch.

PAY ATTENTION TO THE SPELLING RULES

When the stem of the verb ends in **-к, -г, -х, -ж, -ш, -щ, -ч, -ц**, it should never be followed by **"ю"** and **"я"**, and they should be replaced with **"у"** and **"а"**, respectively.

Examples:

у**ч**ить (teach) – я уч**у** – они уч**а**т

ды**ш**ать (breathe) – я дыш**у** – они дыш**а**т

Also note that **vowel "е" is replaced with "ё"** when it becomes stressed in a verb ending.

п**е**ть – мы по**ё**м (we sing)

IRREGULAR VERBS

Just like in English, there are irregular verbs in Russian. Some of them feature completely irregular patterns, while others have changes only in some forms. Below is the table with some of the most common irregular verbs that also highlights the changes to which you should pay attention.

A large group of irregular verbs is formed by **"ова"/"ева"** verbs with the letters replaced by **"у"/"е"** + the corresponding ending.

рис**ова**ть (paint) – я рис**у**ю, ты рис**у**ешь (I paint, you paint)

во**ева**ть (be at war) – я во**ю**ю, ты во**ю**ешь (I'm at war, you're at war)

Note that many **"ова"** verbs are of foreign origin and are easy to understand and memorize.

игнари**ова**ть – ignore

тести**ова**ть – test

регистри**ова**ть – register

организ**ова**ть – organize

With further practice, you'll learn more and will also be able to predict consonant/vowel shifts. For now, let's focus on the basic skill of building regular forms and remembering the widespread irregular ones.

RUSSIAN IRREGULAR VERBS IN THE PRESENT TENSE

	Я	ТЫ	МЫ	ВЫ	ОН/ОНА/ОНО	ОНИ
хотеть want	хочу	хочешь	хотим	хотите	хочет	хотят
бежать run	бегу	бежишь	бежим	бежите	бежит	бегут
давать give	даю	даёшь	даём	даёте	даёт	дают
есть eat	ем	ешь	едим	едите	ест	едят
брать take	беру	берёшь	берём	берёте	берёт	берут
ехать go by vehicle	еду	едешь	едем	едите	едет	едут
видеть see	вижу	видишь	видим	видите	видит	видят
лгать lie	лгу	лжёшь	лжём	лжёте	лжёт	лгут
плакать cry	плачу	плачешь	плачем	плачите	плачет	плачут
искать look for	ищу	ищешь	ищем	ищите	ищет	ищут
жить live	живу	живёшь	живём	живёте	живёт	живут
петь sing	пою	поёшь	поём	поёте	поёт	поют
писать write	пишу	пишешь	пишем	пишите	пишет	пишут
спать sleep	сплю	спишь	спим	спите	спит	спят
бить beat	бью	бьёшь	бьём	бьёте	бьёт	бьют
носить wear	ношу	носишь	носим	носите	носит	носят
просить ask for	прошу	просишь	просим	просите	просит	просят

ходить go, walk, go on foot	хожу	ходишь	ходим	ходите	ходит	ходят
любить love	люблю	любишь	любим	любите	любит	любят
сидеть sit	сижу	сидишь	сидим	сидите	сидит	сидят
идти go	иду	идёшь	идём	идёте	идёт	идут
мыть wash	мою	моешь	моем	моете	моет	моют

REFLEXIVE VERBS IN RUSSIAN

Reflexive verbs correspond to the concept of **"-self"** in English and end in postfixes **"-ся"** or **"-сь"** (for **"я"** and **"вы"**).

Умываться – wash oneself

With reflexive verbs, the subject and the object of the sentence are the same. In "Я одеваюсь – I dress myself", we see that "я" performs the action and is simultaneously the object to which the action is directed.

 To conjugate the verbs that end in postfixes **"-ся"** or **"-сь"**, just remove the postfixes, perform the conjugation, and put them back in place.

Просыпать**ся** (wake up) – просыпать – просыпаю - просыпаюсь

 Note that some verbs lack the concept of a directed action and are reflexive, according to the tradition.

улыбать**ся** – smile, молить**ся** – pray

EXERCISES

1. Group the verbs below into two columns.

включить – turn on, смотреть – watch, улыбаться – smile, строить – build, молчать – keep silent, ездить – go by vehicle, платить – pay, дышать – breathe, лгать – lie, забыть – forgive, ненавидеть – hate, смеяться – laugh, плавать – swim, лежать – lie, петь – sing, нравиться – like, держать – hold, звонить – call, знать – know, ходить – go, рассказывать – tell, видеть – see, есть – eat.

1ST CONJUGATION	2ND CONJUGATION

2. Match the pronouns with the corresponding verb forms.

A.

ПОМНИТЬ – REMEMBER	
RUSSIAN	**ENGLISH**
( ) **1.** я	**A.** помним
( ) **2.** ты	**B.** помню
( ) **3.** мы	**C.** помнит
( ) **4.** вы	**D.** помнят
( ) **5.** он/она/оно	**E.** помните
( ) **6.** они	**F.** помнишь

B.

| ВСТРЕЧАТЬСЯ – MEET EACH OTHER ||
RUSSIAN	ENGLISH
( ) 1. я	A. встречаетесь
( ) 2. ты	B. встречаются
( ) 3. мы	C. встречаюсь
( ) 4. вы	D. встречаемся
( ) 5. он	E. встречаешься
( ) 6. они	F. встречается

C.

| МЫТЬ – WASH ||
RUSSIAN	ENGLISH
( ) 1. я	A. моем
( ) 2. ты	B. мою
( ) 3. мы	C. моет
( ) 4. вы	D. моешь
( ) 5. он	E. моют
( ) 6. они	F. моете

D.

| ВИДЕТЬ – SEE ||
RUSSIAN	ENGLISH
( ) 1. я	A. видим
( ) 2. ты	B. видишь
( ) 3. мы	C. видите
( ) 4. вы	D. вижу
( ) 5. он	E. видят
( ) 6. они	F. видит

3. Choose between two forms of the same verb.

1. **Они ещё (учатся/учимся) в школе или уже в университете?**
   Do they still study at school or at university already?

2. **Я не (носить/ношу) шапки даже зимой.**
   I don't wear hats even in winter.

3. **Андрей не (работают/работает) уже три месяца.**
   Andrew hasn't been working for three months already.

4. **Моё настроение часто (зависят/зависит) от погоды.**
   My mood often depends on the weather.

5. **Что Вы (ищете/ищешь)? Я могу Вам помочь?**
   What are you looking for? Can I help you?

6. **Как давно ты (занимаются/занимаешься) баскетболом?**
   How long have you been doing basketball?

7. **Мы не (обижаем/обижаешь) своих родителей.**
   We don't offend our parents.

8. **Почему ты (стоят/стоишь) под дождём?**
   Why are you standing under the rain?

9. **Летом я всегда (ездят/езжу) на велосипеде.**
   I always go by bike in summer.

10. **Мой дедушка (бреется/бреемся) каждое утро.**
    My grandfather shaves himself every morning.

11. **Ты точно не (хочу/хочешь) пойти с нами?**
    Are you sure you don't want to go with us?

12. **Они не (знают/знает), что делают.**
    They don't know what they're doing.

4. Choose the correct form of the verb.

1. Я _____ посуду два раза в день.
   I wash the dishes twice a day.

   A. моет   **B.** мою   **C.** моем

2. Дети, вы _____ телевизор уже три часа. Сходите поиграйте на улице!
   Kids, you've been watching TV for three hours already. Go play outside!

   A. смотрите   **B.** смотрят   **C.** смотрим

3. Наши гости _____ наш новый адрес?
   Do our guests know our new address?

   A. знаю   **B.** знаем   **C.** знают

4. Мой парень не _____, почему я увлекаюсь аниме.
   My boyfriend doesn't understand why I'm into anime.

   A. понимаю   **B.** понимает   **C.** понимаешь

5. Ты _____, что у мамы завтра день рождения?
   Do you remember that it's Mom's birthday tomorrow?

   A. помнишь   **B.** помню   **C.** помнит

6. Обычно я не _____ днём.
   Usually, I don't sleep during the day.

   A. спят   **B.** спишь   **C.** сплю

7. Мы _____ этот проект для участия в конкурсе.
   We're doing this project to participate in a competition.

   A. делают   **B.** делаем   **C.** делаете

8. Моя соседка по комнате хорошо _____.
   My roommate runs well.

   A. бегает   **B.** бегаю   **C.** бегают

5. Create the right forms of the verbs in brackets in order to complete the sentences.

1. **Малыш, почему ты (плакать)?**   _____
   Why are you crying, baby?   _____

2. **Она вегетарианка и не (есть) мясо.**   _____
   She's a vegetarian and doesn't eat meat.   _____

3. **Бабушка часто (рассказывать) нам о своей молодости.**   _____
   Grandma often tells us about her youth.   _____

4. **Куда вы (ехать) этим летом?**   _____
   Where are you going this summer?   _____

5. **Моя племянница (заниматься) искусством.**   _____
   My niece does art.   _____

6. **Он (платить) своим работникам хорошую зарплату.**   _____
   He pays a good salary to his employees.   _____

7. **Иногда я (брать) детей с собой на работу.**   _____
   Sometimes I take kids to work with me.   _____

8. **Они слишком много (работать) и слишком мало (отдыхать).**   _____
   They work too much and have too little rest.   _____

9. **Ты (выключать) весь свет, когда спишь?**   _____
   Do you turn off all the lights when you sleep?   _____

10. **Дети (строить) что-то из кубиков.**   _____
    Kids are constructing something with their blocks.   _____

11. **Этот щенок так мило (просить) угощение.**   _____
    This puppy asks for a treat in such a cute way.   _____

12. **Вы (лгать), Иван Андреевич, и я знаю это!**   _____
    You're telling lies, Ivan Andreevich, and I know it!   _____

6. Fill in the verbs from the box and create their proper forms in order to complete the conversation. Check and role-play.

CONVERSATION I

помнить смеяться выглядеть смеяться помнить участвовать

A: Алина, почему ты **1)** _____?

B: Ой, подожди минуточку! Я просто не могу остановиться!

A: Ты **2)** _____ уже минут десять. Что там такого смешного в твоём журнале?

B: Ты **3)** _____ Рому, нашего одноклассника?

A: Да, конечно **4)** _____! Он всё ещё такой же странный?

B: Смотри сама. Он **5)** _____ в конкурсе «Мистер Вселенная».

A: Не может быть! Дай посмотреть!

B: Вот, смотри.

A: Ого! Он **6)** _____, как фотомодель! Мне срочно нужно записаться в спортзал. А почему ты смеялась?

B: Это нервы! Я не могу поверить, что отказалась с ним встречаться!

A: Alina, why are you laughing?

B: Oh, wait a minute! I can't stop laughing!

A: You've been laughing for about ten minutes now. What's so funny in your magazine?

B: Do you remember Roma, our classmate?

A: Yes, of course I remember! Is he still so weird?

B: Take a look yourself. He participates in "Mr. Universe" contests.

A: No way! Let me take a look!

B: Here, look.

A: Wow! He looks like a photo model! I urgently need to join a gym. And why were you laughing?

B: Just nerves! I can't believe that I refused to date him!

 **CONVERSATION II**

заканчиваться делать мочь открывать забирать встречаться

A: Привет, Данила! Рад тебя видеть!

B: Привет, Костя! Какой сюрприз! Что ты **1)** _____ в Москве?

A: Я здесь по работе. Я **2)** _____ свой бизнес и **3)** _____ сегодня с партнёрами.

B: Молодец! У тебя будет свободное время?

A: Да, конечно! Моя встреча **4)** _____ в четыре часа, и потом я свободен.

B: Отлично! В четыре я **5)** _____ детей из детского сада.

A: Тогда мы **6)** _____ встретиться в пять, верно?

B: Да, вот мой адрес. Приходи!

A: Hi Danila! Glad to see you!

B: Hi Kostya! What a surprise! What are you doing in Moscow?

A: I'm on business here. I'm opening my own business and meeting my partners today.

B: Good for you! Will you have some free time?

A: Yes, of course! My meeting ends at four o'clock and then I'm free.

B: Great! I'm picking up the kids from the kindergarten at four.

A: Then we can meet at five, right?

B: Yes, here is my address. Come over!

PART III
THE PAST TENSE

The past tense in Russian is needed to talk about past events, either finished or in progress. Good news is that the conjugation of verbs in the past tense is much easier than in the present tense.

The ending depends on the gender of the subject, i.e., the doer of the action. To conjugate a verb in the past tense, remove the ending "-ть" from the initial form and add:

MASCULINE	"-Л"
купить – buy Папа (он) купил продукты на рынке. – Dad (he) bought foodstuffs at the market.	
FEMININE	**"-ЛА"**
приехать – come by vehicle Моя сестра (она) приехала сюда на поезде. – My sister (she) came here by train.	
NEUTRAL	**"-ЛО"**
прийти – arrive Письмо (оно) пришло утром. – The letter (it) arrived in the morning.	
PLURAL	**"-ЛИ"**
фотографировать – take photos Туристы фотографировали собор. – The tourists were taking photos of the cathedral.	

 While with "он", "она", "оно", "они", "мы", and "вы", the number and gender are clear, "я" and "ты" can cause confusion in terms of what gender to choose. Here you should be guided by a simple logic. With "я", the gender depends on the gender of the speaker. With "ты", it depends on the gender of the person to whom you speak.

Я **была** актрисой. – I **was** an actress.
Макар, ты **был** вчера в школе? – Makar, **were** you at school yesterday?

The words that can help you understand that the action took place in the past:

вчера – yesterday

позавчера – the day before yesterday

в прошлом году – last year

на прошлой неделе – last week

в прошлом месяце – last month

в детстве – in my childhood

THE VERBS "БЫТЬ" AND "ЕСТЬ" IN THE PAST TENSE

As you know, the verb "to be – быть" is omitted in the present tense, however, in the past tense it's obligatory.

Дом справа от банка. – The house **is** to the right of the bank.

Дом **был** справа от банка. – The house **was** to the right of the bank.

In constructions **"Здесь есть" – "There is/are"** and **"У меня есть – I've got"**, "есть" is replaced with the corresponding past form of the verb "быть". The conjugation of these verbs in the past is irregular.

У меня **есть** билеты в театр. – I **have** tickets to the theater.

У меня **были** билеты в театр. – I **had** tickets to the theatre.

Masculine – был
В двадцать лет он **был** студентом. – At twenty he **was** a student.
Feminine – была
В детстве у меня **была** любимая игрушка. – In childhood I **had** a favorite toy.
Neutral – было
Солнце **было** высоко. – The sun **was** high.
Plural – были
В комнате **были** дети и их родители. – There **were** children and their parents in the room.

IRREGULAR VERBS

Many irregular verbs form certain patterns in the past tense. However, at this stage it will be best just to remember some of the most common verbs and to improve the skill in the future.

IRREGULAR VERBS IN THE PAST TENSE

VERB	MASCULINE	FEMININE	NEUTRAL	PLURAL
быть be	был	была	было	были
идти go	шёл	шла	шло	шли
нести carry	нёс	несла	несло	несли
мочь can	мог	могла	могло	могли
печь bake	пёк	пекла	пекло	пекли
умереть die	умер	умерла	умерло	умерли
замёрзнуть freeze	замёрз	замёрзла	замёрзло	замёрзли
расти grow	рос	росла	росло	росли

 Note that the past tense is the tense where the difference between imperfective and perfective verbs joins the game. Here are a few more hacks on how to choose the correct aspect.

USE IMPERFECTIVE	USE PERFECTIVE
For actions that were habitual or repeated in the past. Она **ходила** в церковь каждое воскресенье. She used to go to church every Sunday.	**For one-time actions in the past.** Вчера она **сходила** в церковь. Это на неё не похоже. She went to church yesterday. It doesn't look like her.
For actions that lasted in the past. Вчера она весь день **покупала** подарки. She was buying presents all day long yesterday.	**The emphasis is on the result rather than the action itself.** Ты **купила** подарки? Did you buy the presents?
To ask whether the action took place or not. Она вчера **звонила** в головной офис? Я хочу знать, звонить мне или нет. Did she call the head office yesterday? I want to know if I should call or not.	**To ask whether the action took place or not, but in case you knew it had to happen.** Ты **позвонил** в головной офис? Я просила тебя вчера. Did you call the head office? Yesterday I asked you to.

 CONJUGATING VERBS OF DIFFERENT ASPECTS

There is actually no difference in conjugating imperfective and perfective verbs. You should just focus on preserving the parts that make them different. Let's take the verbs "идти – go" and "прийти – to come" as an example.

You know that the verb "идти" is irregular. So, "прийти" will be conjugated according to the same pattern. Just keep the prefix **"при-"** in place.

Они **шли** по просёлочной дороге. – They **were going** along a countryside road.

Они **пришли** вовремя. – They **came** on time.

Let's take a look at another example to make sure you get the idea.

понимать/понять – understand.

The difference is in the suffixes **"-а"** and **"-я"**.

Я никогда не **понимала**, зачем выходить замуж.
I never **used to understand** why marry someone.

Я всё **поняла** и теперь могу объяснить это другим.
I **understood** everything and now I can explain it to others.

 REFLEXIVE VERBS IN THE PAST TENSE.

To create past forms of reflexive verbs, remove the postfix, make the corresponding changes, and put postfix **"-ся"** for masculine and **"-сь"** for feminine, neutral, and plural.

Она **улыбалась**. – She **was smiling**.

улыба**ться** – улыбать – улыба**ла** – улыба**лась**

1. Match the verbs with the images and create masculine or feminine past form, depending on your gender.

(   ) **1.** проиграть   (   ) **5.** простудиться

(   ) **2.** собирать ягоды   (   ) **6.** рисовать

(   ) **3.** помыть посуду   (   ) **7.** покупать

(   ) **4.** готовить ужин   (   ) **8.** считать

A.

E.

B.

F.

C.

G.

D.

H.

2. Match the pronouns with the corresponding verb forms.

A.

ВСПОМНИТЬ – REMEMBER, RECOLLECT	
( ) **1.** он	**A.** вспомнила
( ) **2.** она	**B.** вспомнили
( ) **3.** оно	**C.** вспомнил
( ) **4.** они	**D.** вспомнило

B.

ВОЛНОВАТЬСЯ – WORRY	
( ) **1.** он	**A.** волновалась
( ) **2.** она	**B.** волновался
( ) **3.** оно	**C.** волновались
( ) **4.** вы	**D.** волновалось

C.

ВЫРАСТИ – GROW	
( ) **1.** он	**A.** выросли
( ) **2.** она	**B.** вырос
( ) **3.** оно	**C.** выросло
( ) **4.** мы	**D.** выросла

D.

УСЛЫШАТЬ – HEAR	
( ) **1.** он	**A.** услышали
( ) **2.** она	**B.** услышала
( ) **3.** оно	**C.** услышал
( ) **4.** они	**D.** услышало

3. Choose the correct past form of the verb in brackets.

1. Девушка (села/сел) на второй автобус и (сошёл/сошла) через две остановки.

   The girl took bus number two and went off after two stops.

2. Мои друзья (ездило/ездили) в отпуск в Италию.

   My friends went to Italy for their holiday.

3. Полицейский (приказал/приказала) ему остановиться.

   The policeman ordered him to stop.

4. Фу! Это молоко (испортилось/испортилась)!

   Yuck! This milk has gone bad!

5. Дорогие гости, спасибо что (пришли/пришла)!

   Dear guests, thanks for coming!

6. Мне совсем не (понравилась/понравилось) то кино.

   I didn't like that movie at all.

7. Её двоюродный брат (переехал/переехала) в Венгрию.

   Her cousin moved to Hungary.

8. Кажется, эта птица (сломало/сломала) крыло.

   Looks like this bird has broken its wing.

4. Create the correct past form of the verb in brackets.

1. Раньше мои дети (мочь) смотреть мультики часами. \
   My kids used to be able to watch cartoons for hours.

2. Влад, почему ты (прийти) так поздно вчера? \
   Vlad, why did you come so late yesterday?

3. Света и Данила (встречаться) два года, \
   а потом (расстаться). \
   Sveta and Danila dated for two years and then broke up.

4. Эти цветы (расти) в саду у моей тёти. \
   These flowers used to grow in my aunt's garden.

5. Его дедушка (умереть), когда ему было пять. \
   His grandfather died when he was five.

6. Она (умыться) и (выйти) из ванной. \
   She washed herself and went out of the bathroom.

7. Я оставил яблоко на улице, и оно (замёрзнуть). \
   I left the apple outside and it froze.

8. Ребята, посмотрите, что (принести) \
   Марина Ивановна! \
   Guys, look what Marina Ivanovna has brought!

9. Мой приятель (влюбиться) в мою соседку. \
   My pal fell in love with my neighbor.

10. Спортсмен не (смочь) догнать своих соперников. \
    The athlete was unable to catch up with his rivals.

11. В прошлом году каникулы (закончиться) \
    слишком быстро. \
    The holidays ended too fast last year.

12. Когда мы были детьми, мама (печь) \
    что-нибудь каждое воскресенье. \
    When we were kids, Mom used to bake \
    something every Sunday.

5. Match the sentences with the same-meaning imperfective/perfective verbs.

IMPERFECTIVE	PERFECTIVE
( ) 1. Раньше люди думали, что земля плоская. People used to think that the Earth was flat.	A. Мы вдруг вспомнили, где видели похожую картину. We suddenly remembered where we'd seen a similar painting.
( ) 2. Она никогда не отвечала на вопросы родителей. She never answered her parents' questions.	B. Как ты узнала, что я вру? How did you know I was lying?
( ) 3. Мы сидели и вспоминали студенческие годы. We were sitting and remembering our college years.	C. Коллеги подумали и приняли решение. The colleagues thought for a while and made the decision.
( ) 4. Я всегда знала, что ты лжец! I always knew you were a liar!	D. Прости, что я взяла твои вещи без спроса! I'm sorry I took your stuff without asking!
( ) 5. Оркестр продолжал играть, несмотря на дождь. The orchestra went on playing, despite the rain.	E. Она ответила на вопрос учителя и села. She answered the teacher's question and sat down.
( ) 6. Моя сестра вечно брала мои вещи без спроса. My sister always used to take my stuff without asking.	F. Профессор выпил глоток воды и продолжил. The professor took a sip of water and went on.

6. Choose between the imperfective and perfective verbs and create the past form.

1. Ангелина никогда не (гулять/погулять) в этой части города.
    Angelina has never had a walk in this part of the city.

    _____

2. Ангелина немного (гулять/погулять) по городу и пошла домой.
    Angelina walked about the city a bit and went home.

    _____

3. Настя, он просто пошутил, а ты (думать/подумать), что он серьёзно.
    Nastya, he just joked and you thought he was serious.

    _____

4. Мы (ехать/приехать) всю ночь, и (ехать/приехать) домой только утром.
    We were driving all night and came home only in the morning.

    _____

5. Они долго (решать/решить), как поступить.
    They were deciding for a long time on what they should do.

    _____

6. В детстве он (думать/подумать), что детей покупают в магазине.
    In his childhood, he used to think that babies were bought in a shop.

    _____

7. Они (решать/решили) не продавать дом.
    They decided not to sell the house.

    _____

8. Раньше я (мочь/смочь) бегать часами, а вчера не (мочь/смочь) пробежать даже десяти минут!
    I used to be able to run for hours and yesterday I was unable to run even for ten minutes!

    _____

7. Complete the conversation by choosing the correct form of the verbs. Pay attention that sometimes you'll have to choose between the present and the past tenses. Role-play after checking.

A: Мама, ты не знаешь, куда я **1) (положить)** свои наушники?

B: О, милая, ты вечно **2) (класть)** их в разных местах. Я не **3) (знать)**.

A: В прошлый раз, когда я **4) (спрашивать)**, ты **5) (знать)**!

B: Я не **6) (мочь)** всё время следить за твоими вещами, дорогая.

A: Мама, пожалуйста, помоги мне! Я **7) (опаздывать)** на репетицию!

B: Опять? Ты же **8) (опоздать)** во вторник!

A: Да, и я не **9) (хотеть)** опоздать снова!

B: Ладно, я помогу тебе, но вообще-то ты **10) (мочь)** пойти и без наушников.

1. ( )	A. положил B. положила C. положили	6. ( )	A. могу B. можешь C. могла
2. ( )	A. кладёшь B. кладу C. клала	7. ( )	A. опаздывала B. опаздываешь C. опаздываю
3. ( )	A. знала B. знаю C. знаешь	8. ( )	A. опоздала B. опоздали C. опаздываешь
4. ( )	A. спрашивали B. спрашиваю C. спрашивала	9. ( )	A. хотела B. хочу C. хочет
5. ( )	A. знала B. знаешь C. знаю	10. ( )	A. могла B. могли C. можешь

A: Mom, do you happen to know where I've put my earphones?

B: Oh, dear, you're always putting them in different places. I don't know.

A: Last time when I asked you, you knew!

B: I can't constantly keep an eye on your things, dear.

A: Mom, please, help me! I'm running late for the rehearsal!

B: Again? But you were late on Tuesday!

A: And I don't want to be late again!

B: All right, I'll help you, but actually you can go without your earphones.

PART IV
THE FUTURE TENSE

When creating future tense forms, you should understand what meaning you want to imply, and then choose between an imperfective and perfective verb before conjugating them.

WHEN TO USE IMPERFECTIVE VERBS FOR THE FUTURE

- For future actions that are not implied to be finished;

  Завтра мы **будем убирать** дома. – We **will clean** the house tomorrow.

In this example, there is no emphasis on the completion. Reading the sentence, we don't know if cleaning the house will be finished or not.

- For actions that will be in progress at a certain moment in the future;

  Завтра в пять утра я ещё **буду спать**. – I **will** still **be sleeping** at 5 a.m. tomorrow.

- For actions that will be repeated in the future.

  Я **буду звонить** тебе каждый день. – I **will call** you every day.

WHEN TO USE PERFECTIVE VERBS FOR THE FUTURE

- For actions that are implied to be finished in the future;

  Завтра мы **уберём** дома. – We **will clean** the house tomorrow.

In this example, there is emphasis on completion. Reading the sentences, we understand that they will finish cleaning the house.

- For one-time actions in the future.

  Я **позвоню** тебе, когда приеду домой. – I **will call** you when I arrive home.

CREATING IMPERFECTIVE FUTURE FORMS

To create imperfective future forms, you should conjugate the verb "быть" and add the imperfective infinitive.

Я	буду
Ты	будешь
Мы	будем
Вы	будете
Он, она, оно	будет
Они	будут

Через месяц я **буду заканчивать** проект. – I **will be finishing** the project in a month.

 Note that the verb "быть" can be used independently in the future tense.

Я **буду** рад, если ты придёшь. – I **will be** glad if you come.
Она **будет** в офисе до пяти. – She **will be** in the office until five.

CREATING PERFECTIVE FUTURE FORMS

To create perfective future forms, you should conjugate the perfective infinitive by adding the corresponding endings.

PERSON/PRONOUN	1ST CONJUGATION	2ND CONJUGATION
я	"-ю"	"-у"/"-ю"
ты	"-ешь"	"-ишь"
мы	"-ем"	"-им"
вы	"-ете"	"-ите"
он, она, оно	"-ет"	"-ит"
они	"-ют"	"-ат"/"-ят"

Ты **поможешь** мне завтра с уроками? – **Will you help** me with the homework tomorrow?
Ты **увидишь** там много интересного. – You **will see** many interesting things there.

SOME IRREGULAR FUTURE FORMS

VERB	Я	ТЫ	МЫ	ВЫ	ОН, ОНА, ОНО	ОНИ
мочь to be able to	смогу	сможешь	сможем	сможете	сможет	смогут
помочь help	помогу	поможешь	поможем	поможете	поможет	помогут
дать give	дам	дашь	дадим	дадите	даст	дадут
испечь bake	испеку	испечёшь	испечём	испечёте	испечёт	испекут
спросить ask	спрошу	спросишь	спросим	спросите	спросит	спросят

 Note that sometimes no matter the meaning, some verbs just can't be used with an imperfective meaning, just because they can't denote a process. For example, there is no such form as "я буду мочь", because one either can or can't.

 One more thing to which to pay attention is that some verbs miss the first person future form. For example, you can't say "я победю – I'll win" or "я предупредю – I'll warn," instead you should say "я смогу победить" and "я смогу предупредить."

There are few such verbs and you'll learn to handle them with experience.

EXERCISES

1. Match the perfective verbs with the images and create 1ˢᵗ person singular of the verbs in the future tense.

(   ) **1.** полить цветы

(   ) **2.** прополоть сад

(   ) **3.** выгулять собаку

(   ) **4.** забрать посылку

(   ) **5.** помыть пол

(   ) **6.** сделать макияж

(   ) **7.** закончить картину

(   ) **8.** поутюжить бельё

A.

E.

B.

F.

C.

G.

D.

H.

2. Match the pronouns with the corresponding verb forms.

A.

ОТВЕЧАТЬ – ANSWER	
RUSSIAN	**ENGLISH**
( ) **1.** я	**A.** ответишь
( ) **2.** ты	**B.** ответите
( ) **3.** мы	**C.** отвечу
( ) **4.** вы	**D.** ответим
( ) **5.** он/она/оно	**E.** ответят
( ) **6.** они	**F.** ответит

B.

ПОБЕДИТЬ – WIN	
RUSSIAN	**ENGLISH**
( ) **1.** я	**A.** победите
( ) **2.** ты	**B.** смогу победить
( ) **3.** мы	**C.** победит
( ) **4.** вы	**D.** победят
( ) **5.** он	**E.** победишь
( ) **6.** они	**F.** победим

C.

ПРИЕХАТЬ – ARRIVE	
RUSSIAN	**ENGLISH**
( ) **1.** я	**A.** приедешь
( ) **2.** ты	**B.** приедет
( ) **3.** мы	**C.** приедите
( ) **4.** вы	**D.** приеду
( ) **5.** он	**E.** приедут
( ) **6.** они	**F.** приедем

D.

УВИДЕТЬ – SEE	
RUSSIAN	ENGLISH
( ) **1.** я	**A.** увидишь
( ) **2.** ты	**B.** увидите
( ) **3.** мы	**C.** увижу
( ) **4.** вы	**D.** увидит
( ) **5.** он	**E.** увидим
( ) **6.** они	**F.** увидят

3. Choose between imperfective and perfective future forms.

1. **Завтра я (помогу/буду помогать) маме в саду и не смогу прийти.**
   I'll be helping Mom in the garden tomorrow and won't be able to come.

2. **Я (помогу/буду помогать) тебе, и мы пойдём гулять.**
   I'll help you and we'll go for a walk.

3. **Я (расскажу/буду рассказывать) тебе, но это секрет.**
   I'll tell you, but it's a secret.

4. **Пешком ты (пойдёшь/будешь идти) слишком долго. Я подброшу тебя.**
   You'll be going too long on foot. I'll give you a lift.

5. **Они (будут давать/дадут) нам только один шанс.**
   They'll give us only one chance.

6. **Завтра в это время я уже (буду загорать/позагораю) на пляже.**
   I'll already be sunbathing on the beach at this time tomorrow.

7. **Вы (будете давать/дадите) ему по одной таблетке каждый день в течение недели.**
   You'll be giving him one pill a day for a week.

8. **Если хочешь, мы (испечём/будем печь) твой любимый пирог.**
   If you want, we'll bake your favorite pie.

9. **Завтра ты (пойдёшь/будешь идти) в школу и это не обсуждается!**
   You'll go to school tomorrow and that's out of the question!

10. **Пожалуй, я (буду загорать/позагораю) и пойду домой.**
    I guess I'll sunbathe a bit and go home.

11. Это сложный рецепт. Мы (испечём/будем печь) этот пирог часа два.

It's a difficult recipe. We'll be baking this pie for about two hours.

12. В понедельник профессор (расскажет/будет рассказывать) о древних насекомых.

The professor will be telling about ancient insects on Monday.

4. Match the sentences with the same-meaning imperfective/perfective verbs.

IMPERFECTIVE	PERFECTIVE
( ) 1. Она будет давать тебе кучу советов, просто не обращай внимания. She'll give you tons of advice, just don't pay attention.	A. Этот врач вылечит Вас, не сомневайтесь! This doctor will cure you, don't doubt!
( ) 2. Вы будете завтра помогать в приюте? Will you be helping in the shelter tomorrow?	B. Я дам тебе свой ноутбук в виде исключения. I'll give you my laptop as an exception.
( ) 3. Всю свою жизнь я буду лечить больных животных. I'll be curing sick animals all my life.	C. Я нарежу мясо и оставлю его в маринаде. I'll dice the meat and leave it in the marinade.
( ) 4. Я буду резать ветчину кубиками, ты не против? I'll dice the ham, do you mind?	D. Мы отпразднуем день рождения в торговом центре. We'll celebrate the birthday in the mall.
( ) 5. Когда-нибудь мы будем вспоминать это с улыбкой. Someday we'll be remembering this with a smile.	E. Они не помогут нам бесплатно. They won't help us for free.
( ) 6. Мы будем праздновать день рождения в саду. We'll celebrate the birthday in the garden.	F. Однажды ты вспомнишь обо мне, но будет поздно. One day you'll remember me, but it will be too late.

5. Choose between the imperfective and perfective verbs and create their future forms.

1. Я (любить/полюбить) тебя вечно!

   I'll love you forever!

   _____

2. Она никогда не (любить/полюбить) тебя!

   She'll never fall in love with you!

   _____

3. Она (выбирать/выбрать) духи целую вечность.

   She'll be choosing perfume for ages.

   _____

4. Мне пора. Мама (волноваться/поволноваться).

   I have to go. Mom will be worried.

   _____

5. Мы (плавать/поплавать) и пойдём домой.

   We'll swim for a while and go home.

   _____

6. Дорогой, я быстро (выбирать/выбрать) подарок и вернусь.

   Dear, I'll choose the present quickly and go back.

   _____

7. Они (плавать/поплавать) весь день, если их не остановить.

   They'll be swimming all day if you don't stop them.

   _____

8. Ничего страшного! Она немного (волноваться/поволноваться) и успокоится.

   That's okay. She will worry a bit and calm down.

   _____

6. Complete the conversation by choosing the correct forms of the verbs. Pay attention that sometimes you'll have to choose between the present, the past, and the future tenses. Role-play after checking.

A: Вы не **1) (знать)**, что они здесь строят?

B: Мой сосед вчера **2) (сказать)**, что это **3) (быть)** торговый центр.

A: Ещё один? Они **4) (построить)** ещё один торговый центр? Бред!

B: Согласен с Вами. Я думал они **5) (открыть)** новый тренажёрный зал или салон красоты.

A: Я **6) (думать)**, мы должны пожаловаться, пока не поздно.

B: Но кому? Мне кажется, мэр уже **7) (одобрить)** строительство.

A: Мы **8) (организовать)** митинг!

B: Вы думаете, что это **9) (помочь)**?

A: Конечно! Я **10) (позвонить)** своим друзьям, а вы звоните своим!

1. ( )	A. знали B. узнали C. знаете	6. ( )	A. думает B. думаю C. буду думать
2. ( )	A. сказал B. скажет C. скажу	7. ( )	A. одобрил B. одобрит C. одобряет
3. ( )	A. был B. будет C. будут	8. ( )	A. организовали B. организуете C. организуем
4. ( )	A. построят B. построили C. построит	9. ( )	A. поможет B. помогут C. помогает
5. ( )	A. открыли B. откроет C. откроют	10. ( )	A. позвони B. позвоню C. позвонил

A: Do you happen to know what they're building here?

B: My neighbor said yesterday that it would be a mall.

A: Another one? They will build another mall? Nonsense!

B: I agree with you. I thought they would open a new gym or a beauty salon.

A: I think we should complain before it's too late.

B: But to whom? It seems to me that the mayor has already approved the construction.

A: We'll organize a protest!

B: Do you think it will help?

A: Of course! I will call my friends and you call yours!

PART V
THE IMPERATIVE MOOD

The imperative mood is used to make commands, requests, or give advice. According to the logic, it can be for second person singular – "ты" and second person plural – "вы".

Саша, **напиши** мне, когда приедешь. – Sasha, **text** me when you arrive.
Коллеги, **напишите** мне, когда закончите. – Colleagues, **text** me when you finish.

HOW TO MAKE AN IMPERATIVE FORM?

1. Take a verb infinitive;
2. Define if it's imperfective or perfective;
3. If it's imperfective, make it 3rd person plural present;
4. If it's perfective, make it 3rd person plural future;
5. Remove the ending and leave the stem;
6. Add the corresponding ending.

ENDINGS FOR THE IMPERATIVE MOOD

LAST LETTER OF THE STEM	ENDING	STRESS CHANGE
vowel помог**а**-ют	**"-й"/"-йте"** помога**й**/помога**йте**	no stress change
one or two consonants мо**лч**-ат keep silent	**"-и"/"-ите"** молч**и**/молч**ите**	stress shifts to the ending
One consonant and the infinitive have the stress on the stem, not the ending ст**а**в-ить – place	**"-ь"/"-ьте"** став**ь**/став**ьте**	the stress remains on the stem

Let's follow the steps in two examples

ПОМОГАТЬ – HELP

1. the verb is imperfective;
2. make 3rd person plural present – помога**ют**;
3. remove the ending – помога;
4. the verb ends in a consonant, so add **"-й"/"-йте"** – помога**й**/помога**йте**.

ПРИГОТОВИТЬ – COOK

1. the verb is perfective;
2. make 3rd person plural future – приготов**ят**;
3. remove the ending – приготов;
4. the verb ends in a consonant and the stress in the infinitive is on the stem, so add **"ь"/"ьте"** – приготов**ь**/приготов**ьте**.

IRREGULAR IMPERATIVE FORMS

VERB	2ND PERSON IMPERATIVE	3RD PERSON IMPERATIVE
быть be	будь	будьте
есть eat	ешь	ешьте
ждать wait	жди	ждите
идти go on foot	иди	идите
ехать go by vehicle	едь	едьте
пить drink	пей	пейте
петь sing	пой	пойте
давать give	давай	давайте

бить beat	бей	бейте
вставать get up	вставай	вставайте
писать write	пиши	пишите
просить ask for	проси	просите
взять take	возьми	возьмите

 Note that for making a negative imperative in order to ask someone not to do something, you should just add particle **"не"** before the affirmative form.

Не пей холодную воду! – **Don't drink** cold water!

When using a negative imperative, remember that perfective and imperfective forms can convey different shades of meaning. Like in the example above, the imperfective verb implies an advice against an action, while with perfective verbs, the warning is urgent and very important.

Не забудь полить цветы, а то они засохнут! – **Don't forget** to water the flowers or they will dry out!

Compare with the following, less urgent command that uses the same verb, but in its imperfective option:

Не забывай поливать цветы, пока меня не будет. – **Don't forget** to water the flowers, while I'm away.

HOW TO MAKE THE IMPERATIVE OF REFLEXIVE VERBS?

1. remove the postfix;

2. make an imperative of the verb;

3. if you need 2nd person singular form, add **"-ся"** for forms that end in **"ь"** or **"й"**, and **"-сь"** for forms that end in a vowel;

4. if you need 2nd person plural form, add **"-тесь"**.

Let's analyze an example.

успокоиться – calm down

1. remove the postfix **"-ся"**;

2. make the imperative form for this new verb – успокой;

3. the verb ends in **"й"**, so we add **"-ся"** for 2nd person singular – успокой**ся**;

4. if we need 2nd person plural, we add **"-тесь"** – успокой**тесь**.

There are also ways to express commands or wishes for the 1st and 3rd persons, both singular and plural. Here are a few ways:

1. пусть + subject + 1st or 3rd person verb in present or future.

   Пусть они перестанут шуметь! – **Let them stop** making noise!
   Пусть она едет на машине, а мы пойдём пешком. – **Let her go** by car and we'll go on foot.

2. **Давай (for singular) and давайте (for plural) + plus future verb in the corresponding number.**

   Ребята, **давайте пойдём** в кино! – Guys, **let's go** to the cinema!
   Аня, **давай заведём** кота. – Anya, **let's have** a cat.

How to choose between the perfective and imperfective verb, when making the imperative mood? Follow the same logic as with the indicative mood – use perfective verbs for one-time actions and go for imperfective verbs when talking about continuous actions.

Помогай бабушке, пока будешь у неё. – **Help** your grandma, while staying at her place.

The speaker means that the person should be helping continuously during all the time he/she will be staying at their grandmother's.

Помоги бабушке! Посмотри, какие тяжёлые сумки она несёт. – **Help** your grandma! Look at what heavy bags she's carrying.

The speaker means that the person should help immediately with a certain, one-time action.

EXERCISES

1. Match the verb infinitives with their imperative forms – two for each verb.

VERB	IMPERATIVE FORMS
1. плакать cry	**A.** не шумите
	B. умойся
2. умыться wash oneself	**C.** приготовьтесь
	D. лови
3. шуметь make noise	**E.** не паникуй
	F. ловите
4. паниковать panic	**G.** не плачь
	H. приготовься
5. приготовиться get ready	**I.** не шуми
	J. умойтесь
6. ловить catch	**K.** не паникуйте
	L. не плачьте

2. Match the verbs with the images and make their imperative forms. In order to understand the number of the verb, look at the number of people in the image.

(   ) **1.** написать   (   ) **4.** помириться

(   ) **2.** пить   (   ) **5.** надеть

(   ) **3.** передать   (   ) **6.** купить

A.

D.

B.

E.

C.

F.

3. Fill in the words from Exercise 1 to complete the sentences.

1. Костя и Ваня, сейчас же _____! Вы же братья!
   Kostya and Vanya, make peace at once! You're brothers, after all!

2. Дорогой, _____ мне соль, пожалуйста.
   Dear, pass me the salt, please.

3. Дети, _____ то, что вы видите на доске.
   Children, write what you see on the blackboard.

4. Дедушка, не _____ этот чай, я заварю тебе свежий.
   Grandpa, don't drink this tea. I'll brew some fresh tea for you.

5. Оксана, _____ шапку! На улице мороз!
   Oksana, put your hat on! It's freezing outside!

6. _____ мне мороженое по дороге домой, хорошо?
   Buy me an ice cream on your way home, okay?

4. Choose the correct form of the verb.

1. Егор, (давай/давайте) пригласим твоих родителей на ужин.
   Yegor, let's invite your parents for dinner.

2. Милая, не (рисуй/нарисуй) на стенах.
   Don't paint on the walls, sweetie.

3. Оля, (рисуй/нарисуй) мне домик, пожалуйста.
   Olya, paint me a little house, please.

4. Мама, пусть они (уйдут/уйдём)! Мне страшно!
   Mom, let them go away! I'm scared!

5. (Тренируйся/Потренируйся) чаще и ты станешь сильнее.
   Train more often and you'll become stronger!

6. Ребята (давай/давайте) перестанем спорить!
   Guys, let's stop arguing!

7. **(Вернитесь/Вернись), глупцы! Там опасно!**

    Go back, fools! It's dangerous there!

8. **(Тренируйся/Потренируйся) ещё немного и давай пойдём домой.**

    Train a bit more and let's go home.

9. **Мой вам совет: (оденься/оденьтесь) потеплее завтра.**

    My advice for you: dress warmly tomorrow.

10. **Пусть всё (будут/будет) хорошо!**

    Let everything be fine!

5. Match the sentences with the same-meaning imperfective/perfective verbs.

IMPERFECTIVE	PERFECTIVE
( ) 1. **Я буду поздно сегодня. Не жди меня и ложись спать.** I'll be late today. Don't wait for me and go to bed.	A. **Объясни мне, пожалуйста, я не понимаю это правило.** Explain it to me, please, I don't understand this rule.
( ) 2. **Давайте ему по две таблетки три раза в день.** Give him two pills three times a day.	B. **Дети, поиграйте немного, и мы пойдём домой.** Kids, play a little and we'll go home.
( ) 3. **Не объясняй ей ничего, она всё равно не поймёт.** Don't explain anything to her, she won't understand, anyway.	C. **Дайте мне ещё минутку!** Give me another minute.
( ) 4. **Скажи что-нибудь! Не молчи!** Say something! Don't be quiet!	D. **Подожди меня! Я не успеваю за тобой!** Wait for me! I can't keep up with you!
( ) 5. **Не играйте с этой собакой!** Don't play with this dog!	E. **Замолчи сейчас же!** Shut up right now!

6. Make imperfective forms of the verbs in brackets. Choose between the imperfective and perfective verbs where needed.

1. Карина, не (делать/сделать) больше таких ошибок. _____
   Karina, don't make such mistakes anymore.

2. Не (кричать) на меня, Тарас! _____
   Don't yell at me, Taras!

3. Катя, (делать/сделать) мне кофе, пожалуйста. _____
   Katya, make me a coffee, please.

4. Люди, (улыбаться) чаще! _____
   People, smile more often!

5. Я покажу Вам дорогу. (Идти) прямо _____
   и (повернуть) налево. _____
   I'll show you the way. Go straight ahead and turn left.

6. Если вы не уверены, (просить/спросить) инструктора. _____
   If you're not sure, ask the instructor.

7. Аня, (успокоиться) и (объяснить) всё ещё раз. _____
   Anya, calm down and explain everything one more time.

8. Дети даже не (просить/спросить), _____
   мы не возьмём кота. _____
   Kids, don't even ask, we're not having a cat.

9. Ребята, (рассказывать/рассказать) _____
   нам о своей поездке. _____
   Guys, tell us about your trip.

10. Сынок, пожалуйста, не (ехать) так _____
    далеко в такую погоду. _____
    Son, please, don't go so far in such weather.

11. Я прошу тебя, не (рассказывать/рассказать) _____
    никому об этом. _____
    I beg you, don't tell anyone about it.

12. Игорь, (повторить) ещё раз, чтобы запомнить. _____
    Igor, repeat one more time to remember.

7. Make the correct imperative forms of the verbs in brackets in order to complete the recipes of Russian traditional dishes. Make two forms – one for singular and one for plural. You could use the former to explain the recipe to a friend, while the latter will be good for a wide audience.

RECIPE 1

Сырники

1) (Взять) _____ 200 грамм творога, одно яйцо, две столовые

ложки сахара, три столовые ложки муки и щепотку соли. **2) (Взбить)** _____

яйцо и сахар. **3) (отправить)** _____ яйца с сахаром в блендер.

4) (Добавить) _____ все остальные ингредиенты и

5) (взбить) _____ещё раз. **6) (Сформировать)** _____

небольшие шарики и **7) (сделать)** _____ их плоскими.

8) (Жарить) _____ на среднем огне. **9) (Подавать)** _____

со сметаной, вареньем или мёдом. **10) (Быть)** _____ готовы к наслаждению!

Syrniki

Take 200 grams of cottage cheese, one egg, two tablespoons of sugar, three tablespoons of flour, and a pinch of salt. Whisk the egg and the sugar. Send the eggs with sugar to a blender. Add all the other ingredients and whisk again. Form little balls and make them flat. Fry on medium fire. Serve with sour cream, jam, or honey. Prepare to enjoy it!

 **RECIPE 2**

Салат оливье

1) (Взять) _____ 200 грамм нежирного мяса, пять яиц, две-три картофелины,

одну морковку и банку консервированного горошка. **2) (Сварить)** _____

мясо, яйца, картофель и морковь. **3) (Нарезать)** _____ варёные ингредиенты

кубиками и **4) (перемешать)** _____ всё.

5) (Добавить) _____ горошек и майонез и **6) (перемешать)**

_____ снова. Также можно добавить свежие или

маринованные огурцы и лук. **7) (Есть)** _____ с хлебом и **8) (наслаждаться)**

_____!

Olivier Salad

Take 200 grams of lean meat, five eggs, two or three potatoes, one carrot, and a can of peas. Boil meat, eggs, potatoes, and the carrot. Dice the boiled ingredients and mix everything. Add peas, mayonnaise, and mix again. You can also add fresh or pickled cucumbers and onions. Eat with bread and enjoy!

MISCELLANEOUS PRACTICE – VERBS

1. Match the infinitives with their present, past, future, and imperative forms.

INFINITIVE	PRESENT	PAST	FUTURE	IMPERATIVE
1. разговаривать ( )	**A.** идёшь	**A.** думали	**A.** будешь идти	**A.** пейте
2. думать ( )	**B.** бежим	**B.** пили	**B.** буду разговаривать	**B.** бегите
3. идти ( )	**C.** разговариваю	**C.** звонили	**C.** будем бежать	**C.** иди
4. пить ( )	**D.** звонят	**D.** шёл	**D.** будете звонить	**D.** разговаривай
5. бежать ( )	**E.** думают	**E.** бежали	**E.** будут думать	**E.** звоните
6. звонить ( )	**F.** пьёте	**F.** разговаривал	**F.** будете пить	**F.** думайте

2. Fill in the verbs from Exercise 2.

1. Моя сестра художница. Завтра она едет в Париж и _____

там природу. В прошлом году она _____ портреты. Сейчас

она _____ меня. Надеюсь, будет красиво!

My sister is an artist. She's going to Paris tomorrow and will paint nature there. Last year she was painting portraits. Now she's painting me. I hope it will be beautiful!

2. Мой папа строитель. Сейчас он _____ новый дом. В прошлом

году он _____ небоскрёб. На следующей неделе он

_____ новый бассейн.

My Dad is a builder. He's building a new house now. Last year he was building a skyscraper. Next week he will build a new pool.

3. Дети, вы _____ слишком много сладостей! Вчера вы _____

конфеты целый день и завтра _____ их, если я вас не остановлю!

Kids, you're eating too many sweets! You were eating sweets all day yesterday and you'll be eating them tomorrow if I don't stop you!

4. Я всё время путешествую. Сейчас я _____ в Лондоне, в следующем месяце

_____ в Москве, а в прошлом году я _____ в Далласе.

I'm travelling all the time. I live in London now; next month I will live in Moscow and last year I lived in Dallas.

5. Женя, куда ты сейчас _____? Домой? Я думала, что ты уже _____

и скоро _____ к родителям.

Zhenya, where are you going now? Home? I thought you have arrived already and will soon be going to your parents.

6. Мы с друзьями обожаем спортивные игры! Вчера мы _____ в баскетбол,

завтра мы _____ в футбол, а сейчас мы _____ в хоккей.

My friends and I love sports games! We were playing basketball yesterday, tomorrow we will be playing football, and now we are playing hockey.

3. Choose the correct form of the verb.

1. Ты всё ___ или мне объяснить ещё раз?
   Do you understand everything or should I explain again?

   A. понимает   **B.** понимаешь   **C.** поймёшь   **D.** понимают

2. Наша команда ___ или проиграла?
   Did our team win or lose?

   A. победит   **B.** победили   **C.** победила   **D.** победил

3. Они ___ прийти завтра или нам пригласить их позже?
   Will they be able to come tomorrow or should we invite them later?

   A. смогут   **B.** смогли   **C.** сможет   **D.** сможешь

4. Где ___ ваш медовый месяц? Вы поедете за границу или останетесь в стране?
   Where will your honeymoon be? Will you go abroad or stay in the country?

   A. будут   **B.** был   **C.** были   **D.** будет

5. Мы не виноваты! Мы просто ___ подушками, и ваза упала сама!
   It's not our fault! We were just throwing pillows at each other and the vase fell down on its own!

   A. бросалась   **B.** бросалось   **C.** бросаетесь   **D.** бросались

6. Ого! Твоя собака ___ столько команд!
   Wow! Your dog knows so many commands!

   A. знают   **B.** знает   **C.** знала   **D.** узнают

7. Эдуард Константинович, Вы и правда ___ в Китае?
   Eduard Konstantinovich, have you really been to China?

   A. был   **B.** было   **C.** будет   **D.** были

8. Бабушка ___, если мы не вернёмся к обеду.
   Grandma will be angry if we don't come back by lunch.

   A. будут злиться   **B.** будешь злиться   **C.** будет злиться   **D.** будете злиться

4. Choose between the imperfective and perfective verb and make its correct form, depending on the tense.

1. Олег, пожалуйста, (выключать/выключить) музыку.   _____
   Oleg, turn the music off, please.

2. Они много (помогать/помочь) беженцам.   _____
   They help refugees a lot.

3. В прошлом году мы часто
   (ссориться/поссориться).   _____
   We often had fights last year.

4. Он (делать/сделать) всё, чтобы ты его простила.   _____
   He will do everything for you to forgive him.

5. Я (помогать/помочь), если тебе нужно.   _____
   I will help if you need.

6. Дорогие зрители (готовиться/приготовиться) к шоу!   _____
   Dear audience, get ready for the show!

7. (Стараться/Постараться) ещё раз,
   и у тебя получится!   _____
   Try again and you will succeed!

8. Они продали старую квартиру
   и правильно (делать/сделать)!   _____
   They sold their old apartment and did right!

9. Почему они опять (ссориться/поссориться)?   _____
   Why did they have a fight again?

10. Я предупреждаю тебя, (готовиться/приготовиться)
    к экзамену более серьёзно.   _____
    I warn you: get ready for your exam more seriously.

11. Фонари обычно (выключать/выключить)
    в два часа ночи.   _____
    The lights are usually turned off at 2 a.m.

12. Ты так (стараться/постараться), и у тебя получилось!   _____
    You tried so hard and you succeeded!

5. Choose the correct form of the verb in order to complete the conversation and role-play it after checking.

A: Никита, ты **1) (хотеть)** _____ пойти с нами в поход на этих выходных?

B: С удовольствием, но я не **2) (думать)** _____, что это хорошая идея.

A: Почему? Ты **3) (быть)** _____ занят в это время? Твоей тёте снова нужна помощь?

B: Нет, мы **4) (закончить)** _____ ремонт в её доме неделю назад.

A: Тогда в чём проблема?

B: Ты же **5) (знать)** _____, я ничего не **6) (понимать)** _____ в палатках и прочих вещах.

A: Глупости! Надя тоже ничего не **7) (понимать)** _____, но мы всё **8) (показать)** _____ и

9) (объяснить) _____, теперь она всегда **10) (ходить)** _____ с нами!

B: Что ж, тогда можно попробовать!

1. ( )	A. хочет B. хочешь C. хотела	6. ( )	A. понимал B. понимала C. понимаю
2. ( )	A. думаю B. думал C. думает	7. ( )	A. понимал B. понимали C. понимала
3. ( )	A. будешь B. будет C. были	8. ( )	A. покажем B. показали C. показываем
4. ( )	A. закончила B. закончили C. закончим	9. ( )	A. объяснили B. объясним C. объяснишь
5. ( )	A. знают B. знал C. знаешь	10. ( )	A. ходила B. ходили C. ходит

A: Nikita, would you like to go hiking with us this weekend?

B: I would love to but I don't think it's a good idea.

A: Why? Will you be busy at this time? Does you aunt need help again?

B: No, we finished the renovation of the house a week ago.

A: What's the problem then?

B: You do know that I don't understand anything about tents and other stuff.

A: Nadya used to understand nothing, too, but we showed her everything and explained her everything, and now she always comes with us!

B: Well, I can try then!

CONCLUSION

Hello, winner! Yes, this is exactly what you are after finishing this book! We're almost sure that you are not a grammar guru yet, but every achievement should be judged by the initial goal, and yours was to start building your Russian grammar skills, which you did.

You may not be able to name all the endings and exceptions at the end of the day, but you're 100% more confident, with understanding and more belief in the fact that no matter how hard Russian grammar is, you have the power to master it.

So, what's next? You can and actually should go on chiseling your skills and building new knowledge. With lots of resources for the purpose, including other Lingo Mastery tools, this book still has value to offer. Although much has been learned and the exercises have been completed, it's always a good idea to go back to the contents and take a fresh look at it, to analyze it with a mind that is now packed with more understanding and will consequently help you understand and memorize things better.

We hope this book and the sense of achievement it has given you will be a motivation for you to continue the journey and improve your Russian even more when you feel the progress.

Good luck and hope to see you in other books by Lingo Mastery!

ANSWER KEY

CHAPTER I

PART I

Exercise 1

1. dress (neutral)
2. house (masculine)
3. builder (masculine)
4. flame (neutral)

5. window (neutral)
6. girl (feminine)
7. calendar (masculine)
8. grandfather (masculine)

Exercise 2

Noun	Masculine	Feminine	Neutral
ночь – night		✓	
время – time			✓
герой – hero	✓		
лицо – face			✓
зима – winter		✓	
музей – museum	✓		
станция – station		✓	
шоколад – chocolate	✓		
фотография – photo		✓	
январь – January	✓		
кошка – cat		✓	
море – sea			✓
стол – table	✓		
кафе – café			✓
машина – car		✓	
дядя – uncle	✓		
апрель – April	✓		
семья – family		✓	
друг – friend	✓		

Exercise 3

1. собаки
2. яйца
3. музеи
4. глаза
5. дети
6. пальто
7. фотографии
8. деревья

Exercise 4

1. здания
2. газеты
3. слова
4. братья
5. каши
6. цветы
7. письма
8. истории
9. люди
10. лимоны
11. поезда
12. вечера

Exercise 5

Always singular	Always plural
вода, мебель, посуда, молоко, любовь	деньги, очки, брюки, часы, ножницы

1. мебель
2. ножницы
3. любовь
4. очки
5. часы
6. вода
7. молоко
8. брюки
9. деньги
10. посуда

Exercise 6

Conversation I

1. общежития
2. комнаты
3. адреса
4. семьи
5. студенты
6. ключи
7. кровати
8. кресла
9. трамваи

Conversation II

1. мальчики
2. сыновья
3. доктора
4. визы
5. ножи

PART II

Exercise 1

1. B – молока
2. E – одноклассника
3. A – машины
4. F – вопроса

5. C – печенья
6. G – собаки
7. H – игрушек
8. D – Саши

Exercise 2

1. D
2. G
3. A
4. B

5. C
6. F
7. E
8. H

Exercise 3

1. B
2. C
3. A
4. B

5. A
6. C
7. C
8. B

Exercise 4

1. России
2. окна
3. карманов
4. Макара
5. чая
6. мужей

7. дочерей
8. словаря
9. жены
10. поля
11. шампанского
12. платья

Exercise 5

1. химии
2. маме
3. директору
4. подруге
5. Кате

6. тёте
7. щенку
8. телефону
9. пенсионеру
10. Максиму

Exercise 6

1. C
2. F
3. A
4. G

5. H
6. B
7. E
8. D

Exercise 7

1. прабабушке
2. телеведущему
3. детям
4. племяннику
5. стене

6. студентам
7. морю
8. парикмахеру
9. коллегам
10. другу

Exercise 8

1. знаю
2. забыла
3. ненавижу
4. видеть

5. любит
6. помнишь
7. слышали
8. любит

Exercise 9

1. под
2. про
3. на

4. через
5. в
6. за

Exercise 10

1. incorrect/лицо
2. incorrect/путешествие
3. correct

4. incorrect/скатерть
5. correct
6. correct

Exercise 11

1. D – зеркалом
2. G – друзьями
3. A – водителем
4. B – королём

5. C – зимой
6. H – ложкой
7. E – утром
8. F – учениками

Exercise 12

1. над
2. под
3. перед
4. за
5. между

Exercise 13

1. B – водой
2. A – ветеринаром
3. A – ночью
4. C – раковиной
5. C – музыкантом
6. A – родителями
7. B – камнями
8. C – автором

Exercise 14

1. location – кроватью
2. direction – кровать
3. location – холмом
4. direction – холм
5. location – шкафом
6. location – коробками
7. direction – шкаф
8. location – коробками

Exercise 15

1. волосах
2. крыше
3. приключениях
4. лице
5. урагане
6. магазине

Exercise 16

1. каше
2. карточку
3. штанах
4. карточке
5. кашу
6. школу
7. штаны
8. школе

MISCELLANEOUS PRACTICE – NOUNS

Exercise 1

1. без имени/имён
2. после урока/уроков
3. о чувстве/чувствах
4. внутри игрушки/игрушек
5. с молоком (no plural form)
6. о герое/героях
7. в игре/играх
8. к светофору/светофорам
9. на мотоцикле/мотоциклах
10. через ворота (no singular form)
11. на концерт/концерты
12. с вершины/вершин

Exercise 2

1. к светофору
2. с молоком
3. внутри игрушек
4. без имён
5. после уроков
6. на мотоцикле
7. на концерт
8. о чувствах
9. с вершины
10. в играх
11. по мобильному
12. через ворота

Exercise 3

1. B
2. A
3. D
4. A
5. A
6. C
7. D
8. B

Exercise 4

Conversation 1: брата, брате, брату, братом
Conversation 2: детьми, детей, детям, детях
Conversation 3: кошку, кошки, кошку, кошки, кошке, кошках, кошки

CHAPTER II

PART I

Exercise 1

1. F – она
2. D – они
3. A – оно
4. B – мы

5. G – он
6. E – она
7. H – вы
8. C – оно

Exercise 2

1. B
2. C
3. A

4. B
5. C
6. B

Exercise 3

1. тобой
2. мне
3. нас
4. него, его
5. ней

6. Вам
7. им
8. меня
9. вас
10. тебе

Exercise 4

1. 1 – ней, 2 – неё
2. 1 – ними, 2 – них

3. 1 – нём, 2 – него
4. 1 – него, 2 – ним

Exercise 5

Conversation I

1. тебе
2. тебе
3. меня
4. тебе

5. меня
6. она
7. ей
8. тебя

Conversation II

1. ей
2. она
3. её
4. нас
5. её

6. ей
7. ей
8. она
9. мне
10. тебя

PART II

Exercise 1

1. A – твой костюм
2. C – ваша подруга
3. D – его шляпа
4. H – моя книга
5. E – наши билеты
6. B – Ваши документы
7. F – их дети
8. G – его лучи

Exercise 2

1. A
2. B
3. C
4. C
5. A
6. A
7. B
8. A

Exercise 3

1. его, его
2. их, их
3. её, её
4. его, его

Exercise 4

1. C
2. A
3. A
4. D
5. A
6. B
7. C
8. D

Exercise 5

1. твоей
2. вашей
3. моей
4. Вашим
5. нашими
6. моей
7. твоих
8. моего
9. нашим
10. ваших
11. мой
12. твоему

Exercise 6

Conversation I

1. Вашим
2. моим
3. мой
4. наша
5. нашей
6. его
7. мою
8. его
9. твоим
10. наш

Conversation II

1. наших
2. ваших
3. нашей
4. моя
5. их
6. наших

Conversation III

1. тебе
2. мой
3. моего
4. твоём
5. нашей
6. твоим
7. моим

PART III

Exercise 1

1. both
2. свою
3. её
4. both
5. своих
6. -
7. both
8. both
9. её
10. both
11. -
12. его

Exercise 2

1. C
2. A
3. B
4. B
5. D
6. C
7. A
8. D

Exercise 3

1. собой
2. себя
3. себе
4. себе
5. себя
6. собой

Exercise 4

1. сами
2. себя
3. себе
4. само
5. себе
6. сам

Exercise 5

1. F – друг другу
2. A – друг без друга
3. C – друг о друге
4. B – друг с другом
5. E – друг на друга
6. D – друг друга

Exercise 6

CLOSE TO THE SPEAKER, RELATED TO THE PRESENT	FAR FROM THE SPEAKER, RELATED TO THE PAST
это сообщение, эти макароны, эта актриса, этот роман, эта юбка, эти здания, это лекарство	та ошибка, тот преступник, те спортсмены, то здание, то пальто, тот компьютер, та история

Exercise 7

1. тем зданиям
2. этом романе
3. это лекарство
4. тем преступником
5. ту ошибку
6. этой актрисой
7. тем спортсменам
8. ту историю

Exercise 8

Conversation I

1. это
2. то
3. себе
4. себя
5. сама
6. свою

Conversation II

1. себя
2. себя
3. свой
4. друг друга
5. сам

PART IV

Exercise 1

1. D
2. A
3. C

4. F
5. B
6. E

Exercise 2

1. D
2. F
3. B

4. A
5. C
6. E

Exercise 3

1. B
2. A
3. C
4. B

5. C
6. A
7. B
8. C

Exercise 4

1. чей
2. чьего
3. какой

4. которого
5. каких
6. какого

Exercise 5

1. чём
2. какое
3. чьим
4. кого
5. каком
6. каком

7. которым
8. чьего
9. кому
10. какими
11. скольких
12. котором

Exercise 6

1. B
2. A

3. D
4. C

Exercise 7

1. B
2. C
3. A
4. A

5. C
6. A
7. C
8. B

Exercise 8

I. никого, не с кем

II. ничего, никаких, ни о чём

III. ни о каком, ничем

PART V

Exercise 1

1. D
2. E
3. A
4. G

5. B
6. H
7. C
8. F

Exercise 2

1. на которой
2. вместо которых
3. с которой
4. на чьи

5. на каком
6. для кого
7. о чём
8. после которого

Exercise 3

1. B
2. A
3. B
4. C
5. B
6. A
7. C
8. B

Exercise 4

1. D
2. A
3. F

4. B
5. C
6. E

Exercise 5

1. где-то
2. что-то
3. куда-то
4. какой-то
5. кто-нибудь
6. как-то

Exercise 6

1. кто-нибудь
2. кто-то
3. куда-то
4. что-то

5. куда-нибудь
6. какой-то
7. что-то
8. какой-то

Exercise 7

1. B
2. A
3. C
4. C

5. A
6. A
7. B
8. A

Exercise 8

Conversation I

1. сколько
2. как-то
3. какой-нибудь
4. что

5. который
6. что-нибудь
7. что-нибудь

Conversation II

1. что-то
2. куда-то
3. который
4. что-то

5. что
6. чей
7. где-то
8. какой-то

MISCELLANEOUS PRACTICE – PRONOUNS

Exercise 1

1. 1 – C – g
2. 2 – E – b
3. 3 – A – d
4. 4 – G – a
5. 5 – B – c
6. 6 – D – f
7. 7 – F – e

Exercise 2

1. друг с другом
2. себя
3. ничей
4. твоя
5. что
6. нечего
7. свой, сама
8. ту
9. тебе
10. себе, сколько

Exercise 3

1. B
2. C
3. A
4. A
5. C
6. B
7. C
8. A

Exercise 4

1. мне, своей, её
2. твоего, его
3. ничего
4. кому
5. него
6. чьих-то
7. нашим, им
8. никого

Exercise 5

1. меня
2. которое
3. какой
4. что-то
5. оно
6. сколько
7. Вы
8. какая-то
9. что
10. чём-то

CHAPTER III

PART I

Exercise 1

1. B
2. G
3. F
4. H
5. A

6. E
7. I
8. C
9. J
10. D

Exercise 2

1. F
2. H
3. B
4. A

5. G
6. C
7. D
8. E

Exercise 3

Masculine	Feminine	Neutral	Plural
зелёный, сложный, сладкий, мягкий, добрый, толстый, красный	опасная, лучшей, светлую, слабой, здоровая	знаменитое, обычное, медленное, счастливое, тёмное	интересные, модные, холодных, круглые, молодым

Exercise 4

1. тёплое
2. быстрая
3. важные
4. злая
5. грязное
6. горький

7. квадратные
8. худая
9. счастливое
10. младшая
11. жаркие
12. серьёзное

Exercise 5

1. B
2. A
3. B
4. C

5. C
6. A
7. B
8. B

Exercise 6

1. старого
2. маленькой
3. острым
4. хорошей

5. высокой
6. следующую
7. лучшего
8. мягкого

Exercise 7

1. молод, красив
2. голодна
3. коротка

4. счастливы
5. испорчено
6. спокоен

Exercise 8

Conversation I

1. интересных фильмов
2. романтических комедий
3. научными фильмами
4. скучными вещами
5. новому ноутбуку
6. большом экране

Conversation II

1. красной сумке
2. квадратном столе
3. красной сумки
4. синим пакетом
5. детскими вещами
6. новых футболок
7. жёлтыми яблоками
8. яблочного пирога

Exercise 9

Text I

1. новом районе
2. хорошее место
3. зелёных парков
4. милых кафе

5. городском автобусе
6. маленькую машину
7. большая машина

Text II

1. солёный суп
2. острого перца
3. хорошим мужем
4. честным человеком
5. новому рецепту
6. готовую еду

PART II

Exercise 1

1. выше, самый высокий
2. моложе, самый молодой
3. холоднее, самый холодный
4. грязнее, самый грязный
5. сильнее, самый сильный
6. толще, самый толстый

Exercise 2

1. C – f
2. F – a
3. D – h
4. B – g
5. G – e
6. H – b
7. A – c
8. E – d

Exercise 3

1. самый страшный
2. более удобный
3. увереннее
4. самый весёлый
5. худший
6. проще
7. самый жаркий
8. мягче

Exercise 4

1. B
2. A
3. A
4. C
5. B
6. A
7. B
8. C

Exercise 5

1. короче
2. слабее
3. самый милый/милейший
4. младшим
5. добрее
6. серьёзнее
7. раньше
8. холоднее/более холодной
9. самое сложное
10. дешевле
11. самый вкусный
12. старше

Exercise 6

Conversation I

1. лучше
2. лучшая
3. быстрее
4. умнее
5. лучше
6. лучшие

Conversation II

1. реже
2. ближе
3. менее престижный
4. лучшее
5. терпеливее
6. старше

MISCELLANEOUS PRACTICE – ADJECTIVES

Exercise 1

1. C
2. A
3. B
4. D

Exercise 2

1. B
2. A
3. B
4. A
5. C
6. A
7. C
8. B

Exercise 3

A

1. интересным
2. интересное
3. интересные
4. интересную

B

1. белое
2. белая
3. белые
4. белого

C

1. любимой
2. любимого
3. любимое
4. любимой

Exercise 4

1. дорогие
2. популярной
3. вкусной
4. здоровой
5. особенного
6. простые
7. обычные
8. экзотических
9. вкусное
10. несложное

CHAPTER IV

PART I

Exercise 1

1. F
2. B
3. E
4. D
5. A
6. C

Exercise 2

1. D
2. F
3. H
4. A
5. B
6. G
7. C
8. E

Exercise 3

1. C
2. A
3. D
4. B

Exercise 4

A. 1 – imperfective 2 – perfective
B. 1 – perfective 2 – imperfective
C. 1 – perfective 2 – imperfective
D. 1 – perfective 2 - imperfective
E. 1 – imperfective 2 – perfective

Exercise 5

1. покупаю
2. купила
3. делать
4. захочет
5. показалось
6. буду работать
7. хотела
8. поверила
9. сделал
10. казалось
11. поработали
12. верила

Exercise 6

1. A
2. C
3. B
4. B

5. B
6. C
7. A
8. B

PART II

Exercise 1

1st conjugation	2nd conjugation
улыбаться, молчать, платить, забыть, смеяться, плавать, лежать, знать	включить, смотреть, строить, ездить, дышать, лгать, ненавидеть, петь, нравиться, ходить, держать, звонить, ходить, видеть, есть

Exercise 2

A
1. B
2. F
3. A
4. E
5. C
6. D

B
1. C
2. E
3. D
4. A
5. F
6. B

C
1. B
2. D
3. A
4. F
5. C
6. E

D
1. D
2. B
3. A
4. C
5. F
6. E

Exercise 3

1. учатся
2. ношу
3. работает
4. зависит
5. ищете
6. занимаешься

7. обижаем
8. стоишь
9. езжу
10. бреется
11. хочешь
12. знают

Exercise 4

1. B
2. A
3. C
4. B

5. A
6. C
7. B
8. A

Exercise 5

1. плачешь
2. ест
3. рассказывает
4. едите
5. занимается
6. платит

7. беру
8. работают, отдыхают
9. выключаешь
10. строят
11. просит
12. лжёте

Exercise 6

Conversation I

1. смеёшься
2. смеёшься
3. помнишь
4. помню
5. участвует
6. выглядит

Conversation II

1. делаешь
2. открываю
3. встречаюсь
4. заканчивается
5. забираю
6. можем

PART III

Exercise 1

1. A – проиграл/а
2. C – собирал/а
3. G – помыл/а
4. B – готовил/а

5. F – простудился/лась
6. H – рисовал/а
7. E – покупал/а
8. D – считал/а

Exercise 2

A	B	C	D
1. C	1. B	1. B	1. C
2. A	2. A	2. D	2. B
3. D	3. D	3. C	3. D
4. B	4. C	4. A	4. A

Exercise 3

1. села, сошла
2. ездили
3. приказал
4. испортилось

5. пришли
6. понравилось
7. переехал
8. сломала

Exercise 4

1. могли
2. пришёл
3. встречались, расстались
4. росли
5. умер
6. умылась, вышла

7. замёрзло
8. принесла
9. влюбился
10. смог
11. закончились
12. пекла

Exercise 5

1. C
2. E
3. A

4. B
5. F
6. D

Exercise 6

1. гуляла
2. погуляла
3. подумала
4. ехали, приехали

5. решали
6. думал
7. решили
8. мог, смог

Exercise 7

1. B
2. A
3. B
4. C
5. A

6. A
7. C
8. A
9. B
10. C

PART IV

Exercise 1

1. D – полью
2. A – прополю
3. H – выгуляю
4. G – заберу

5. B – помою
6. F – сделаю
7. C – закончу
8. E – поутюжу

Exercise 2

A	B	C	D
1. C	1. B	1. D	1. C
2. A	2. E	2. A	2. A
3. D	3. F	3. F	3. E
4. B	4. A	4. C	4. B
5. F	5. C	5. B	5. D
6. E	6. D	6. E	6. F

Exercise 3

1. буду помогать
2. помогу
3. расскажу
4. будешь идти
5. дадут
6. буду загорать

7. будете давать
8. испечём
9. пойдёшь
10. позагораю
11. будем печь
12. будет рассказывать

Exercise 4

1. B
2. E
3. A
4. C
5. F
6. D

Exercise 5

1. буду любить
2. полюбит
3. будет выбирать
4. будет волноваться

5. поплаваем
6. выберу
7. будут плавать
8. поволнуется

Exercise 6

1. C
2. A
3. B
4. A
5. C

6. B
7. A
8. C
9. A
10. B

PART V

Exercise 1

1. G, L
2. B, J
3. A, I

4. E, K
5. C, H
6. D, F

Exercise 2

1. B – напиши
2. E – пей
3. A – передай

4. D – помиритесь
5. F – надень
6. C – купи

Exercise 3

1. помиритесь
2. передай
3. напишите
4. пей
5. надень
6. купи

Exercise 4

1. давай
2. рисуй
3. нарисуй
4. уйдут
5. тренируйся

6. давайте
7. вернитесь
8. потренируйся
9. оденьтесь
10. будет

Exercise 5

1. D
2. C
3. A
4. E
5. B

Exercise 6

1. делай
2. кричи
3. сделай
4. улыбайтесь
5. идите, поверните
6. спросите

7. успокойся, объясни
8. просите
9. расскажите
10. едь
11. рассказывай
12. повтори

Exercise 7

Recipe 1

1. возьми/те
2. взбей/те
3. отправь/те
4. добавь/те
5. взбей/те
6. сформируй/те
7. сделай/те
8. жарь/те
9. подавай/те
10. будь/те

Recipe 2

1. возьми/те
2. свари/те
3. нарежь/те
4. перемешай/те
5. добавь/те
6. перемешай/те
7. ешь/те
8. наслаждайся/тесь

MISCELLANEOUS PRACTICE – VERBS

Exercise 1

1. C – F – B – D
2. E – A – E – F
3. A – D – A – C

4. F – B – A – A
5. B – E – C – B
6. D – C – D – E

Exercise 2

1. будет рисовать, рисовала, рисует
2. строит, строил, будет строить
3. едите, ели, будете есть

4. живу, буду жить, жил
5. едешь, приехал, поедешь
6. играли, будем играть, играем

Exercise 3

1. B
2. C
3. A
4. D

5. D
6. B
7. D
8. C

Exercise 4

1. выключи
2. помогают
3. ссорились
4. сделает
5. помогу
6. приготовьтесь

7. постарайся
8. сделали
9. поссорились
10. готовься
11. выключают
12. старался

Exercise 5

1. B
2. A
3. A
4. B
5. C

6. C
7. C
8. B
9. A
10. C

MORE BOOKS BY LINGO MASTERY

We are not done teaching you Russian until you're fluent!

Here are some other titles you might find useful in your journey of mastering Russian

√ Russian Short Stories for Beginners

√ Intermediate Russian Short Stories

√ 2000 Most Common Russian Words in Context

√ Conversational Russian Dialogues

But we got many more!

Check out all of our titles at **www.LingoMastery.com/Russian**

Made in the USA
Monee, IL
20 October 2024

68379298R00136